Woman
of Letters

Woman
of Letters

Irène Némirovsky
AND
Suite Française

With a short story, "The Virgins,"
by Irène Némirovsky

Edited by Olivier Corpet
and Garrett White

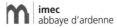

ABOVE
Irène Némirovsky, ca. early 1920s

OPPOSITE
Irène Némirovsky at the Regina Hotel,
Nice, France, ca. 1920

ABOVE
Irène Némirovsky, n.d.

OPPOSITE
Irène Némirovsky, ca. late 1930s

TABLE *of*
Contents

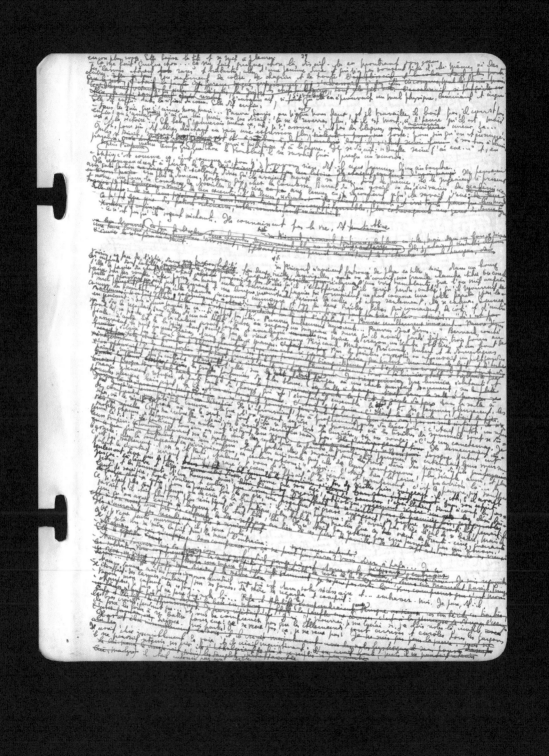

PREFACE

The origin of this book, and the exhibition it accompanies, can be traced
back to the launch of Irène Némirovsky's *Suite Française* in the United States
in April 2006. It was at the New York reception, sponsored by the publisher
Alfred A. Knopf and the Cultural Service of the French Embassy, that the
handwritten manuscript of *Suite Française* was displayed publicly for the
first time. And it was also there that we met—Olivier Corpet, founder and
director of the Institut Mémoires de l'Édition Contemporaine (IMEC),
the French foundation entrusted with the Némirovsky archive, and David
G. Marwell, director of the Museum of Jewish Heritage–A Living Memorial
to the Holocaust (MJH).

Even in our contemporary world, with its unlimited sensory opportunities,
the experience of viewing the manuscript of *Suite Française* offers something
that cannot be matched in any other medium. Just as an aroma or a particular
passage of music can unlock a potent memory, so too can the presence of
an extraordinary object connect us to a vivid experience of imagination and
awareness. We decided right there that IMEC would join with the Museum
of Jewish Heritage in New York City to create an exhibition about Irène
Némirovsky, and that we would place the manuscript of *Suite Française* at
its center.

Némirovsky's manuscript has immense power to communicate. Not only
is it the original and final draft of a major novel, but it is also compelling
evidence of the process of writing, containing, as it does, the author's strike-
outs and emendations, her notes on structure, and the plotted arcs of her
story. Knowing the personal history of the author—Némirovsky was writing
in the last days of her life, fearing that she was running out of paper and
time—one is tempted to search in this manuscript for clues to the context
in which she wrote and to her emotional and mental state. One notes the
cramped, seemingly hurried lines of script, and can imagine them to be
tiny capillaries—blue veins of ink—through which Némirovsky desperately
poured out her imagination and her talent. But even if one, perhaps wisely,
resists the temptation to bring to this remarkable artifact one's knowledge
of Némirovsky's fate, it has an undeniably elemental quality. As we discussed
how the project might take shape, we agreed that it would also have to
include the suitcase in which the manuscript had rested for more than fifty
years, before Némirovsky's daughter, Denise Epstein, opened and read it

for the first time. We believed that the suitcase, like the manuscript, would have an exceptional ability to communicate a story.

In fact, the history of literature is punctuated with the discovery of suitcases and trunks that contained lost or stolen manuscripts. Such discoveries hold the potential of transforming—enriching or perhaps shattering—our previous conception of a writer's work. The suitcase can, therefore, be a symbol of promising and unpredictable potential. But under other circumstances, those of war, exile, and dislocation, for example, the suitcase can also be a potent symbol of flight, desolation, and terror. We need only think about the suitcases found by the thousands in the death camps, abandoned there, emptied of their contents. Representing an irretrievable loss, the suitcase can stand as a silent and compelling testimony of past crimes and tragedy.

Given its rich potential as symbol and metaphor, the suitcase can serve as the quintessential museum artifact, and we are grateful beyond words to Denise Epstein for lending it to the exhibition. She had to overcome her fear that the suitcase, which means so much to her, would somehow attract unhealthy attention once elevated to a museum artifact. As the only object that Némirovsky left behind when she was deported to Auschwitz, and as the container that held the unknown manuscript of *Suite Française* for so many years, the suitcase has enormous power, conveying a dual legacy—personal and literary—and a dual fate—tragic and redemptive. We were certain that both of these remarkable artifacts, the manuscript and the suitcase together, would allow the viewer to encounter the physical and symbolic embodiment of an impossibly poignant story about memory and forgetting, about mothers and daughters, about legacy and loss.

The notion of our two institutions working together on this project seemed natural since, despite our different focus, we both have an abiding devotion to preserving memory and passing it on. IMEC is dedicated to safeguarding literary, artistic, and publishing archives and making them available to scholars and the public, while MJH is devoted to telling the story of twentieth-century Jewish history and the Holocaust. Although we choose different lenses through which to view the past, we each take great care in how we present it. The story of how the exhibition and this book came to life is, therefore, one of complementary institutions engaging in a common project, which throughout has been defined by uncommon cooperation.

In confronting the intellectual challenge of relating the complex and difficult history that surrounds Irène Némirovsky and her story, one realizes the importance of understanding the context in which she lived and wrote. We have endeavored to tell the story of a real woman, who lived at a particular time and place, and one who was confronted with unimagined—and unimaginable—challenges. Our interest was not hagiography but rather history with all of its nuance and texture.

When we decided to pursue this project, we knew that it might well be controversial for any institution to undertake, and even more so for a Jewish museum. We knew by reading her work, and by going through her personal correspondence and papers, that Némirovsky could be said to have exhibited a measure of ambiguity with respect to her identity as a Jew, and we knew that she had converted to Catholicism in 1939. We knew as well that her early works contained Jewish characters who represented difficult and distasteful stereotypes, and that she had been criticized for the company she kept and for the publications in which her work appeared. However, she was neither the only Jew nor indeed the only Jewish writer at the time to have displayed such ambiguities, and one must use extreme caution before retrospectively passing judgment.

Since the publication of *Suite Française*, a few critics have raised serious charges against Némirovsky, accusing her of self-hatred and even at times of anti-Semitism. They note that she included no Jewish characters in *Suite Française*, suggesting that she cared nothing for their fate. Some even suggest that her works somehow contributed to a kind of enabling of those who ultimately killed her. Ironically, these critics have created of Némirovsky the very kind of one-dimensional stereotype that they accuse her of portraying in her novels. Some individuals have even extended their attacks on her and her memory to the next generation by suggesting that the story of the discovery of *Suite Française* was at best exaggerated and at worst fabricated—that commercial hype was responsible for the success of the book, and not the author's talent or the poignancy of her story.

In spite of the concerns that have been raised and despite the attacks, we remain confident that Némirovsky's story is indisputably a Holocaust story; she was deported to Auschwitz, where she perished. And we are equally confident that hers is a Jewish story. Not only was she taken to Auschwitz with a Jewish star stitched to her blouse, but she also identified as a Jew, and her story echoed and reflected the stories of many Jews who shared her fate. Némirovsky's sense of herself as a Jew and the way she behaved under exceptional circumstances may have had ambiguous elements, but there was no ambiguity in the way she was perceived by her enemies or in the nature of her ultimate fate.

We believe that anyone who reads the work of Irène Némirovsky and understands the context in which she wrote, anyone who understands and appreciates literature, will reject the baseless and destructive attacks that have been leveled against her and her memory. In reading her work, one encounters the output of a greatly talented writer, whose books and stories reflect both the inner world of her experience and personal history and the outer world in which she lived and wrote. And we believe that anyone who encounters Némirovsky's daughter, Denise, and hears her relate the discovery of *Suite Française* will question neither its authenticity nor its impact. We also note here that Némirovsky never finished *Suite Française*, and that her life was cut short as she entered what would surely have been her most mature and productive period. One can only wonder what she would have produced had she not been murdered by the Nazis.

The following pages offer enrichment for anyone who has read Irène Némirovsky's work. Her short story, "The Virgins," is published here for the first time in English. It originally appeared in French in a weekly magazine under a pseudonym, on the very day that Némirovsky arrived at the Pithiviers camp. We can imagine her countrymen reading this last work to be published in her lifetime, two days before she was crammed into the train bound for Auschwitz and a dark future that was not yet known to her. Those who read and loved *Suite Française* will be thrilled to find the notes that Némirovsky had prepared for *Captivity,* the third but never written section of that masterful novel. A comprehensive chronology by Némirovsky's French biographers, richly illustrated with never-before published family photographs, provides a glimpse into her life and a context for her work. Finally, an interview with Denise Epstein gives perspective and insight into the remarkable and riveting story of her mother, *a woman of letters.*

OLIVIER CORPET
Director
Institut Mémoires de l'Édition Contemporaine

DAVID G. MARWELL
Director
Museum of Jewish Heritage –
A Living Memorial to the Holocaust

Irène Némirovsky and her mother, Anna, ca. 1916

ABOVE
Irène and her father, Léon Némirovsky,
Nice, France, ca. 1920

OPPOSITE
Irène Némirovsky at the Regina Hotel,
Nice, France, ca. 1920

ABOVE
Anna and Léon Némirovsky,
Nice, France, n.d.

OPPOSITE TOP
Irène Némirovsky and her parents,
Léon and Anna, n.d.

OPPOSITE BOTTOM
Irène Némirovsky and her father, Léon, n.d.

LEFT
Léon and Anna
Némirovsky,
Fontainebleau,
France, n.d.

OPPOSITE
Irène Némirovsky
and her mother,
Anna, n.d.

ABOVE TOP
Irène Némirovsky, ca. 1920

ABOVE BOTTOM
Irène Némirovsky, 1920

OPPOSITE
Léon and Anna Némirovsky,
Nice, France, n.d.

TOP LEFT
Irène Némirovsky, n.d.

LEFT
Anna Némirovsky, n.d.

OPPOSITE
Léon Némirovsky, n.d.

ABOVE
Irène Némirovsky, St. Jean-de-Luz,
France, n.d.

OPPOSITE
Irène Némirovsky in costume, n.d.

Denise and Élisabeth Epstein, ca. 1938

Interview *with* Denise Epstein

BY OLIVIER CORPET AND
EMMANUELLE LAMBERT

The story of the publication of Suite Française *by your mother, Irène Némirovsky, begins with a suitcase. Could you tell us about this suitcase, where you found it and what it contained?*

Irène Némirovsky and Denise, Élisabeth, and Michel Epstein, Hendaye, France, 1939

During our time in Issy-l'Évêque, first at the hotel and then at the house, I was completely unaware of the existence of the suitcase. I never even saw it when I was a child. The suitcase only played a part when my father, Michel Epstein, was arrested. That was when my father took it out of the bedroom; it was closed and I had no idea what was in it, except that it contained things that were obviously precious to him. The suitcase remained in the house at Issy while we were at the *Kommandantur* [German Police Headquarters] at Le Creusot. That was when the incident with the German officer happened that I have often described. I can't recall what his rank was, but he was obviously someone very high up. He let my sister and me go, because he hadn't received orders to arrest children, at least, not at that point in 1942. The orders regarding the arrest of children—I think it's still important to remind people of this—came from the French authorities, by individuals such as [René] Bousquet and [Maurice] Papon, who decided at the time that it was too expensive for France to bear the financial burden of so many future orphans! They used the argument of "Christian charity" as an excuse not to separate families, so arresting children with their parents was an act of kindness according to them, but this German officer, well, he refused to do it. It was therefore a kind of gift to us, the gift of life, but almost more a curse than a blessing, in a way.

My father was thrown into prison in Le Creusot and we went back to our house in Issy-l'Évêque with our nanny, Julie Dumot. The German officer made it clear that we shouldn't drag our feet. So we only stayed there for three or four days. I remember that we were there long enough to receive a letter from my father, from prison, asking for some wine, needles and thread, and soap so he could wash his clothes, and he sent us his love. He hadn't yet been sent away...I seem to recall that it took two or three days to find a car, since no one in the village had one. Just as our father was being taken away, he said to me, "There is a suitcase with mama's notebook in it. You must always keep it with you."

Denise and Élisabeth Epstein,
Hendaye, France, 1939

Irène Némirovsky with Denise and Élisabeth Epstein, ca. 1938

*A "notebook," that was exactly what
he called it?*

Yes, it was called a notebook because "file" was a word I might
not understand. Afterwards, it became simply the "manuscript"
to me. He told me I must always keep it with me because it was
"mama's notebook," that's all…And when we went on the run
in the middle of the night, after he had entrusted the suitcase to
me, I carted it around as best I could, because it was very heavy.
Even empty, it was heavy. But there wasn't much in it; in fact, the
manuscript was the heaviest thing. It contained very little clothing,
and the little leather briefcase we took wasn't very big either. And
I couldn't even fit my doll into it. I made such a fuss! A fuss over
my doll…We can be so silly!

Did you open the suitcase before taking it with you?

Yes, to pack some clothes for Élisabeth and me. And in fact, the suitcase never left my side, not during the whole time we were in hiding, not until the end of the war. At that time, it was handed over to a notary, along with the will and the photographs, when I was put into the boarding school of Notre-Dame-de-Sion… I didn't actually know what was in it at that time. I myself was a minor, and it was Julie Dumot, our guardian, who took care of all that. I got the suitcase back when I reached legal majority at 21. After that, it stayed with me until the day I gave it to my daughter, who had nothing that had belonged to her grandparents. Perhaps I also didn't want to have to look at it any more… At times, I even nearly gave it a kick, because after the publication of *Suite Française* it had become something of a cult object to the readers, while to me, it was something completely different… Of course, it was a suitcase, and a handsome one; it must have been very beautiful at one time. It had my grandfather's intials engraved on it, "L N" [Léon Némirovsky]. It's also very odd to see how well the material has held up, since it must have been around the world and back again with him.

Julie Dumot, at the Avot family home near Versailles after World War II

How long did you keep the suitcase with you?

Until Élisabeth reached her legal majority, when I had the right to get back everything I wanted, and so was able to keep the promise I made to my father to take very special care of the suitcase.

Denise and Élisabeth Epstein, ca. 1938

The suitcase, originally belonging to Léon Némirovsky, in which the manuscript for *Suite Française* was found (11.2 x 19.3 x 16.5 inches)

Did you open it?

Yes, of course, at the beginning, since it was necessary to place the Will and other documents with the notary. As for the manuscript, I got it back at the same time as the suitcase and the other papers.

When did you read the manuscript for the first time?

Years and years later, really. First of all because we thought that the rightful owner of the suitcase should be the one who opened it. We waited for her to come back for such a long time. We knew, but we didn't want to accept it, so we fantasized for many years. The explanation of why she hadn't returned that worked the best was telling ourselves that she had amnesia. It was absurd, but we thought, "They have amnesia and are probably in Russia," because when the camps were liberated, each country tried to repatriate its own citizens, and my parents were Russian. We thought all kinds of things like that, and it went on for years, to the point that I was already a mother myself when one day I ran after a woman in the street because I was convinced it was mama. Things like that make it difficult to open a suitcase.

Irène and Denise, ca.1931; Irène and Élisabeth, ca. 1938; Michel and Denise, n.d.

Do you remember when you finally really opened it?

In about 1955–56, to take out some photos.

Photos that were in the suitcase?

Yes. I took them out very quickly, because on the whole, they were symbolic of happy times—except for one.

Except for one?

Irène Némirovsky, n.d.

Yes, there was a terrible picture that most probably was taken for the census, a little photo for an identity card. Mama's face looked completely drained and she had such a sad expression; her hair was all disheveled, in a hairnet, because mama had a mass of very curly hair—like Élisabeth, you know—and so she used a hairnet. But the other ones were photos that really help you to go on living. We could console ourselves that they had some very happy times. Of course, her life had many ups and downs. She was very lonely as a child; she experienced the Russian Revolution, then went into exile. Next came a very wild period, which will surely be considered shocking, but it was a time that made her very happy. It was while she was a student, and she went to endless parties and balls. And then she had a family, and her talent exploded with her first book, and then, afterwards, the real tragedy—she was thirty-nine when she was taken…All that is quite something as a life's journey.

When did you open the famous notebook that you now call the "manuscript"?

Well, it was one day in 1975 or thereabouts, perhaps it was even in 1980. I had a flood at home; my washing machine overflowed. I always needed to have that manuscript, that notebook, where I could see it and touch it; I didn't open it, but I could touch it, and almost breathe it in...And when I saw the water damage, I realized that it was actually the only thing I had left. So Élisabeth and I opened it together, closed it again, opened it again, closed it again. We took a very, very long time before deciding to find out what was written inside. In fact, I was obsessed by the color, the color of the ink, the traditional color that I began searching for, and which I have only just managed to find again—South Seas Blue. She could only write with that particular ink, and I remember the scene she made when it was impossible to get hold of that South Seas Blue. In fact, there are some passages of *Suite Française* that are written in black ink, if I remember correctly. In any case, for her it was essential, just like the pens that my father bought for her and which each had little nicknames. I never did find them. In the final note she wrote to us in pencil from the police station, mama asked for them!

So it was your father who typed the manuscript of Suite Française?

Yes, he typed a part of *Suite Française*, which was his own version, his proofread version.

Michel Epstein and Irène Némirovsky, n.d.

Was that first typed copy also in the suitcase?

No, it wasn't in the suitcase; it was with the other papers [from Albin Michel], with sweet little notes written in the margins, things like "that's silly."

So your father was the first person to read your mother's work?

Always, for everything. We found the beginning of *Chaleur du sang [Fire in the Blood]* in the suitcase, the two or three pages my father had typed...and there was more in another archive at IMEC. The rest of the handwritten manuscript was discovered by mama's biographers, Olivier Philipponnat and Patrick Lienhardt, after the publisher Albin Michel desposited its own historical archives at IMEC. The material had been entrusted to the good care of André Sabatier, mama's friend and editor at Albin Michel. It was amazing to be able to link up my part with theirs: not a single word was missing. And at the same time, I also found some little notebooks, the kind that school children use, in which my father had translated a biography of Pushkin from Russian, undoubtedly for my mother.

Where did you find those little notebooks?

Denise and Élisabeth Epstein, 1945

Well, it was later on, after we'd got back everything we'd been able to take with us the night we left...I had no idea at all what had been taken from Issy-l'Évêque... We ran away with just the bare essentials in the middle of the night, headed for the station where we could get the train to Bordeaux. But afterwards, certain things that were in our house in Issy-l'Évêque went with Julie Dumot. I have no idea where she stored them all. I was still only a child, and she never told me about anything she did...I'm sure that there were many things that disappeared, because long after the war ended, in the 1960s, I went to see a family near Bordeaux—without telling them I was coming—a family where I'd been with Julie Dumot, probably one of her cousins, I can't really remember very well any more.

A family where you had been hidden?

Denise Epstein, 1950

So when your sister reached her legal majority, you began the task of trying to recover your heritage that had been dispersed?

A purse that belonged to Irène Némirovsky

Did you both go there?

Where was the suitcase while you were in boarding school?

Hidden or just stayed with for a while before moving on, I can't remember... Anyway, I saw some things from my house, including a little stool that I immediately grabbed because I associated it with mama, she used it when she was writing... I took it and said, "This belongs to my mother." And I know there must have been an enormous amount of things like that scattered about, things that were even capitalized on because someone once tried to pass himself off as the author of one of mama's manuscripts that had been found. I discovered all of this when I began to gather together all the papers and my father's proofread version of *Suite Française.*

At first, everything was kept at my house and we made copies for each of us. But it was a time when Élisabeth needed to distance herself, in her own way. She didn't want to hear anything about it, and she also considered me the guardian of everything because I had known them. I was the older sister, with a great difference in our ages, seven and a half years, and because she had no memory of them, she said. We virtually didn't have the same past, because we were separated very early on, right after the war, in fact. At that time, a Family Panel was set up, with the publisher, Albin Michel, the bank where my father had been an executive, and the *Société des gens de lettres* [Writer's Guild] too, because we were wards of the court. It was terrible, they had to do something with us, we had no one, no apartment, no family left; they chose a private Catholic boarding school for us, Notre-Dame-de-Sion, located on the rue Notre-Dame-des-Champs in Paris.

Yes, but Élisabeth got into trouble a lot *[laughter]*, and got herself expelled rather quickly. In the meantime, our guardian, Julie Dumot, took off in a hurry for the United States and no one ever heard from her again. Our other guardian, whom I never met, also left for the USA. So the only people who were left were the publishers, the bank, and the *Société des gens de lettres.*

With the notary; I had no choice.

When and why did you finally say to yourself: You know, I really should take a good look and see what's in that suitcase?

I began opening it little by little. And I was afraid…What held us back for a long time, both Élisabeth and me, was the idea that it was a personal diary. I started by leafing through it, but soon the tears began to flow, very quickly at first. I closed it again because I was afraid that the ink would fade. I actually wonder if there aren't certain sections that are a bit blurred because of my tears. And it was just then that we got to know about IMEC through Jean-Luc Pidoux-Payot, who was my sister's best friend, and Jean Gattégno, Director of the Literary Division at the Ministry of Culture, another friend of Élisabeth's, who was his editor.

We both thought that IMEC was exactly what we needed to rescue our mother from oblivion. But that decision also made me realize that I couldn't give away the manuscript without knowing what was in it. So that's how it happened. And of course, at the time, Élisabeth was working on her novel *Le Mirador [The Watchtower]*. I finished transcribing the manuscript before the publication of *Le Mirador*. So Élisabeth did read *Suite Française*, only she didn't want it to be published then, that's all. It took me two and a half years to transcribe it.

So you began by reading it and then you transcribed it?

No, I can't even say that I read it. Instead, I would compare it to the work of a scribe who copies without taking anything in, without understanding it, with only one goal: to leave nothing out, not even a single comma. It was difficult. And from time to time there were certain funny things that happened, for example, the fact that I didn't see *Dolce*, the second part of *Suite Française*. I thought that there was just *Tempête en juin [Storm in June]* quite simply because so many blank pages separated the two large sections of *Suite Française*; the third part, *Captivité [Captivity]*, was only in outline form…It was so painful…I didn't understand what it was at first…But by the end, yes, I did—I knew it was a novel about the mass exodus from Paris in 1940. But I knew the real name of each character—I recognized them all! There was only one I wasn't sure about, the porcelain collector, but Olivier Philipponnat and Patrick Lienhardt made the connection between that character and a very right-wing journalist of the time. But they were the ones who made the link, not me.

The first two manuscript pages of *Suite Française*

At the time, did you transcribe everything—the entire novel and the rest of the notes?

Once we decided to entrust all the documents to the IMEC archives, I wanted to keep a copy for myself, so I transcribed all of it before sending everything to them.

Did you give it to your sister to read as you were transcribing it?

First I copied out *Storm in June*, and then I stopped, because at the same time, I was doing research at the Bibliothèque Nationale [French National Library] in order to find all my mother's short stories and interviews that had been printed at the time, and that work also took a very long time. And so I closed the notebook, then opened it again later on, and, well, that was when I chanced upon *Dolce*, since I had originally stopped when I'd come to the blank pages which, as I said before, actually separated the two sections. It was truly difficult—yes, more difficult than exciting. In fact, I would even say that it was extremely painful. And when I saw *Dolce*, I started transcribing again, and then the manuscript went from my house in Toulouse to join the rest of the IMEC archives. I was in tears when the representative from IMEC came to collect it.

How was the decision made to publish Suite Française?

I recall that you, Olivier, were the first person to read it after me and Élisabeth. You read my transcription and told us that we had to publish it. In fact, I still hadn't considered the possibility that it could be published, and besides, Élisabeth didn't want it to be published.

The leather-covered notebook manuscript of *Suite Française*.

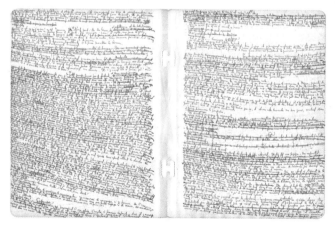

Manuscript pages from *Suite Française*.

Why not?

Élisabeth Epstein, age 16, Versailles, 1953

And besides, Élisabeth was an editor…

So there were several motivating forces: one that made you open the suitcase, one that made you read the manuscript, and finally the one that led you to publish the manuscript?

Difficult to say. It is possible that at that particular time in her life, when she was right at the point of trying to discover the absent mother she had never really known, and also when she was expressing her own need to write, she might have felt caught up in someone else's writing, even though she herself wrote magnificently well; but I think that mainly she found it a bit slapdash—even if that's not exactly the right term—and she wasn't entirely wrong, because it's true there are passages that mama would have certainly reworked…There you have it. But mama wrote the words "The End." That was also something I had qualms about: knowing what a perfectionist she was, would mama have allowed it to be published as it was? You only have to look at the manuscript of *Suite Française*, especially *Storm in June*, to see all the scribbling and scratching out. There are fewer corrections in *Dolce*, since she had the feeling, almost a premonition, that she wouldn't have the time to edit it. It was a credit to Élisabeth that she had reservations, and perhaps that was a factor too; as for me, I was really too involved in the story, too emotionally involved, by the images that these pages awakened in me.

And a talented one! I had absolute faith in her. Moreover, I considered *Suite Française* as unfinished; the manuscript wasn't complete, in fact…did we therefore have the right to publish it just as it was, incomplete? It was truly a question of conscience, and so it remained as it was…It lived in my dresser drawer. There you have it.

As far as publishing the manuscript goes, all it took was a chance meeting [in 2004] in Toulouse in a bookshop called *Ombres Blanches*, where I am a regular customer. Myriam Anissimov had come to talk about her biography of Romain Gary. I had known her for a long time. We had met Myriam when she interviewed us for Grasset's rerelease of some of our mother's works in the collection they call *Les Cahiers Rouges*. At the time [in 1985], she published a very long article in the newspaper *Le Matin*. Obviously, we got to know each other during the course of the interview, so I went to hear her speak because I liked her. After the lecture, we chatted in a way that was, well, I wouldn't call it polite chit-chat, but we spoke casually of this and that:

"What have you been doing?" "Not much really, but I have a clear conscience now that I've had my mother's last works published." I was thinking of the short stories I'd given to a local publisher in Toulouse, who also held a post with the Sables publishing house. Then I told her, "Now, sadly, all I have left is one manuscript, but it is unpublishable…" And when she heard that, she persisted. "A manuscript by your mother!" "Yes," I replied, "but it isn't complete; she only finished two volumes out of five." Then she asked what it was about, and I said, "It's about the mass exodus [from Paris in June 1940] and the arrival of the German occupying troops in a French village." And that was when she finally exclaimed, "I'm calling my publisher."

But I didn't know who her publisher was. I had only ever had any contact with Denoël in the past, when Élisabeth was in charge of one of their collections, *Présence du futur*. I wasn't familiar with the publishing house anymore; I didn't even know who was running it at the time. And so I got a phone call from someone called Olivier Rubinstein, Denoël's director, who was practically in tears on the phone. "I'm begging you," he said, "will you at least let me read it?"—to which I replied, "But look, it isn't finished, and if you do read it, I want you to look at it as an editor, just as an editor would read an author, and not the way you would look at a victim." And he agreed. Two days later, he asked me to come to Paris, and as a result, I didn't even have time to think about it. I explained my doubts to him, especially my hesitations regarding a related subject, the file that contained documents on the relationship between my mother and her publisher, Albin Michel, some of which were later included at the end of *Suite Française*. First of all, these documents did not actually belong to us. They belonged to the publisher who had kindly given them to us when Élisabeth was doing research for her book, *Le Mirador*. Secondly, I showed these papers to Olivier Rubinstein not so that he might publish them, not at all, but so he could get to know my parents, so he could understand how much my father loved my mother, something that comes through in these letters, which are often tragic. So I showed him all of the documents with that in mind, and he was the one who said they had to be published. We contacted Francis Esménard, the president of Albin Michel, since he was the trustee of the file, and asked for permission to use it. He admitted that his father had entrusted the file to him years before and that he had never opened it. Then he very generously gave us the permission we had requested.

Michel Epstein and Irène Némirovsky, n.d.

It also seems that he had no memory of the material that you mentioned earlier in this interview, the boxes that were later found in Albin Michel's archives at IMEC.

If he did, he never told us about them. I always remained on the sidelines where the world of publishing was concerned. It had been a long time since I'd lived in Paris, and it wasn't really a world in which I felt at ease. I think that if Élisabeth had known about those boxes, she certainly would have used them, and she would have told me about them. I don't think anyone knew that more boxes existed. So that was how something that had waited for years and years happened in the space of forty-eight hours. And afterwards, I was completely overwhelmed by everything that followed. But that's another story, another chapter: the continuing story of *Suite Française.*

The continuing story of the opening of the suitcase…

Yes, the continuing story of the opening of the suitcase, indeed. Which is almost as heavy to bear, at times, as the suitcase was itself.

Do you have any regrets at all about having forced yourself to open the suitcase?

Original manuscript outline for
Storm in June, part one of *Suite Française*

That depends on the day, but on the whole, I am happy that my mother is now recognized all over the world, in thirty-five countries, and that she is studied in secondary schools, in high schools, in universities. I knew there would be a price to pay for that. I hadn't anticipated what that price would be, I think, because my mind doesn't work in that convoluted way, but I was quite sure that one day there would be consequences, and there are, because certain things do upset me. For example, there is all the publicity around every word mama might have written, and the mountain of projects that are a result of *Suite Française,* in the movies, in the theater, at the Opera. All of it is wonderful, and I am extremely grateful to everyone who played a part in the rebirth of my mother.

Out of all of these projects, I am particularly interested in the one organized by the Deschamps family, who are going to mount a production of *Le Bal [The Ball]* at the Opéra Comique in Paris. The Deschamps, in fact, are the Péricand family of *Suite Française.* It was Jérôme Deschamps who recognized his family. It was very funny, because I have never told anyone the real names of the characters in the book simply because, on the whole, they aren't very likeable, and also because future generations shouldn't have to pay for the actions of their parents. I never reveal any names. But since he was the one who recognized them, I confirmed it. "Yes," I said, "it is your family."

Suite Française has now become rather a cult book and has brought true recognition of your mother's talent. Are you not afraid that its success might perhaps overshadow the rest of her work?

That doesn't seem to be the case, at least, not for the moment! Everything has been reissued and is being read both in France and abroad, and this is certainly thanks to *Suite Française*. Not all of her books have the same merit, of course, but readers are interested in how novels evolve. As for her style, that is unique. But of course, some of mama's books I like less than others.

Cover of the French edition of *Suite Française*, 2004

For example?

Among the ones I like the most are the ones that describe characters who are Russian, unbalanced, in exile…On the other hand, I do not feel at all comfortable when she describes the French bourgeoisie. I don't really like that, and personally, I feel I have far more in common with people who are a bit lost, a bit hopeless. I feel much more at home with them than with people who have lunch every day at the same time, who respect certain rituals, like making social calls on Sundays.

What about David Golder*?*

Illustrated reprint edition of *David Golder*, ca. 1939

With *David Golder* I had some problems at various stages in my life, personal problems, moral problems. I am a post-Shoah Jew, and it was very painful when I began doing research at the Bibliothèque Nationale. Not knowing where I would find mama's articles, I was forced to leaf through vile newspapers. However, if you analyze these publications more carefully, you can see the dichotomy that existed in these newspapers between the political sections, which were often horrible, and the literary sections, where you could find all sorts of big names. There is a lot of talk now about mama and the campaign against her because of her supposed anti-Semitism, but Stefan Zweig published in *Gringoire* just like all the other important authors of the time; there were many great writers, both Jews and non-Jews!

Irène Némirovsky, ca. 1940

But how could she have used such and such a term, I wondered… It was very difficult. I also had to try to imagine myself back in that time, but that meant getting emotionally involved… Let's just say that I really adore some of mama's books, like *La Vie de Tchékhov [The Life of Chekhov]*, which no one ever talks about despite the fact that it's wonderful, and also *Le Vin de solitude [The Wine of Solitude]*, *Les Mouches d'automne [Snow in Autumn]*, or *Les Chiens et les Loups [Dogs and Wolves]*… Some of the later works, like *Les Biens de ce monde [All Our Worldly Goods]*, I find enjoyable, but, well… I think she wanted to immerse herself in the French bourgeoisie because she admired it and she thought people were happier if they led a balanced, calm, sensible life, even though that kind of life isn't very enjoyable, in my opinion. I don't like that sort of thing. I prefer the night, the world of darkness.

Do you get the impression that there has been some confusion in the way that Suite Française *has been received? If not in France, at least abroad?*

A map of France with the main cities and rivers drawn by Denise Epstein on a page in her mother's notebook for *Suite Française*

After having traveled a great deal, I have the impression that each country has interpreted *Suite Française* according to its own real-life experiences. It is therefore impossible to generalize. England, for example, had difficulty in accepting the debacle of the French army, given the fact that just weeks after the German offensive began, the soldiers either surrendered or ended up as part of the mass exodus, heading not to the front, but in the opposite direction. While in Britain, the English lived through a very tough war. London was bombed but everyone stayed. They were very harsh in their criticism of the way the French soldiers fled, but I have told them that the important thing about *Suite Française* is that they don't understand what it is like to be in an occupied country, and that makes all the difference in the attitude adopted towards *Suite Française* and what then happened to mama. In Finland, what impressed them was the fact that my mother spent some time in their country and that in one of her short stories she describes an enormous famous bookshop in Helsinki, which I visited, and where, as mama said at the time—she was seventeen years old then—she found all the French literature she loved so much. And so the Finnish had a perspective on this woman as someone who had lived in their country for a while. In Sweden, it was the same: mama, or her family in any case, had certainly stayed at Stockholm's famous Grand Hôtel. I was shown through it from top to bottom, since they were convinced that all wealthy Russians fleeing the 1917 Revolution would have surely stayed there. As for the Spanish, I have often asked why they were so enthusiastic, since they are the ones who buy all of mama's books and by a large margin. Well, it's strange, because when I ask them that question, for them, the answer is death; the connection they make between a Russian Jew and themselves is death. So I have learned something about each country.

And what about the United States?

The late author and editor Élisabeth Epstein Gille in her office at Éditions Julliard, 1990

Denise Epstein reviewing the manuscript for *Suite Française* at the IMEC archive and research facility, l'Abbaye d'Ardenne, Normandy, France, 2004

In the United States, even though I did my best to explain that it was American historians like Robert O. Paxton who were the first to work on the history of Vichy and the Jews in France, they were still scandalized. Of course, in America, a large portion of the audience was Jewish, and when I went to the United States in 2005, it was the time when there were troubles in the suburbs in France, and they very nearly offered me political asylum *[laughter]*. It was really quite incredible; they couldn't actually grasp the idea of collaboration, and I had to explain very carefully that a country is never either all black or all white, and that even though there had actually been many denunciations in France, there were also people who saved our lives…

Each country truly has a unique perspective, but in France, this book has made many rather extraordinary things possible. It made it possible for families to talk to each other, to be open. This also happened in the Netherlands, and I will always remember one elderly couple I met. The gentleman was really in a sad state; he had gone blind.

They came to hear me speak one evening at the French Institute, and the next day I ran into them in a bookshop. "Thank you," the woman said to me, in tears, "because as soon as we got home last night, my husband asked me to open a suitcase and to take out some old notebooks, and he asked me to read them to him, which I did all through the night." And so, even if only because of a few things like that, I believe it was worth opening my mother's notebook that my father entrusted to my care.

The above interview was conducted at the IMEC office in Paris, France, February 21, 2008, and read and amended by Denise Epstein.

Translated from the French by Sandra Smith

ABOVE
Irène Némirovsky's Aunt Victoria Margoulis
(her mother Anna's younger sister) with her
children Iakov and Elena, n.d.

OPPOSITE
Irène Némirovsky, ca. 1924

ABOVE
Irène Némirovsky with her parents
Léon and Anna and maternal grandparents
Jonas and Bella Margoulis in the south
of France, ca. 1922–23

OPPOSITE
Michel Epstein and Irène Némirovsky,
ca. 1926

CHRONOLOGY

OF THE LIFE OF

IRÈNE NÉMIROVSKY

by Olivier Philipponnat and Patrick Lienhardt

1648

JUNE 10
Instigated by the Cossack leader Bogdan Chmielnicki, a pogrom in the town of Nemirov, Ukraine, claims the lives of six thousand Jews.

1791

Empress Catherine II imposes the Pale of Settlement, restricting Russian Jews to the western region of the empire, with the exception of the largest cities, notably Kiev.

NOTE
This chronology was adapted by the authors from their biography, *La Vie d'Irène Némirovsky* (Grasset-Denoël, 2007). Quotations in italics are from the writings of Irène Némirovsky. —Trans.

1847

Birth in Odessa of Irène's maternal grandfather, Jonas Margoulis, ↑ also called Iona or Johann, who would recite passages from French writers like Racine, Voltaire, and Hugo to his granddaughter. *"He was the only one who spoke perfect French. He said 'ma petite fille' with a strong stress on the last syllable to emphasize it."* (Journal, 1934/ Archive Némirovsky/IMEC)

1854

Birth in Ekaterinoslav of Rosa Chtchedrovitch, known as Bella, ↓ Irène's maternal grandmother. *"Poor woman—small, slim, frail... with a face as faint as an old photograph, its features blurred, yellowed, faded with tears."* (Journal, 1934/IMEC)

1868

SEPTEMBER 1

Birth in Elisavetgrad of Leonid (Léon) Borisovitch Némirovsky, ↓ Irène's father, *"an obscure Jewish boy"* orphaned at the age of ten. He started out as a hotel messenger, then a factory worker in Lodz, a warehouse manager in Odessa, an entrepreneur in the match business, and ended up a banker. *"The only one I felt really related to by blood, by my anxious soul, by my strength and my weakness."* (Journal, 1934/IMEC) Nicknamed "The Arab," like Pushkin, because of his complexion. His daughter Irène inherited his coloring.

c. 1875

Birth of Irène's mother, Anna Margoulis. ↑ She would later call herself Fanny or Jeanne, to sound French, and change her birth certificate to make herself younger by twelve years. *"I remember my mother very well. How odd that even now I can't write that word without hatred."* (Journal, 1934/IMEC)

1893

Birth of Victoria (Vika) Margoulis, Anna's sister, whom Irène always thought of as her own sister. The two corresponded until 1940. *"My aunt was pretty, with soft skin and a slim figure, and as simple as a flower."* ("Le Sortilège" ["The Spell"], published in *Gringoire*, February 1, 1940)

c. 1902

Marriage of Anna Margoulis and Leonid Némirovsky.

1903

FEBRUARY 11

Birth in Kiev of Irina (Irène) Irma Némirovsky, the only child of Anna Margoulis and Leonid Némirovsky, nicknamed "Irotchka" or "Irinouchka." A fifty-year-old French governess, called "Zézelle," would be put in charge of her education. *"During my childhood, she represented my refuge, my light… She was the only one in the world I truly loved."* (Notebook, 1934/ IMEC) Zézelle taught her French nursery rhymes and "La Marseillaise." *"I spoke French before I spoke Russian."* (Interview, *Les Nouvelles littéraires*, April 6, 1940)

Left to right, Irène Némirovsky, "Zezelle," and Victoria Margoulis, n.d.

1905

OCTOBER 17

Following the First Russian Revolution, Tsar Nicholas II signs the October Manifesto, granting equality and basic civil rights to all, and setting up the Duma as the main legislative body.

OCTOBER 18

Pogroms against Jews break out in Kiev and Odessa. Irène, wearing a Russian Orthodox cross around her neck, is hidden behind a bed by Macha, the family cook. *"Hear that? That's a window being broken. Can you hear the glass shattering? That's stones being thrown against the walls and the iron shutters of the shop. That's everyone laughing. And there's a woman screaming as if her insides were being ripped out. What's going on?"* (*Les Chiens et les Loups,* 1940) After these attacks, 200,000 Russian Jews choose to go into exile.

C. 1910

The Némirovsky family, including Irène's maternal grandparents, Jonas and Rosa Margoulis, move to 11 Pushkin Street, in the upmarket Pechersk district of Kiev. Up until 1914, the family goes numerous times to Paris, as well as to the spa towns of Vichy, Divonne, Plombières, and Vittel, the Côte d'Azur (Cannes, Nice), and the Côte Basque (Biarritz). Seaside summer vacations were taken at Yalta and Aloucha in the Crimea. Irène is raised by tutors, one of whom is a Socialist revolutionary.

1911

Dressed in a costume like the one worn by Sarah Bernhardt, Irène recites Rostand's *The Eaglet* at a charity event for the Maison Française in Kiev, attended by the Governor-General Vladimir Sukhomlinov. ↑ *"I was very nervous to find myself opposite this person who for us symbolized terror, tyranny, and savagery. To my great surprise, I saw a charming man who looked like my grandfather, and had the gentlest eyes you'd ever seen."* (Interview, Radio-Paris, June 2, 1933)

JULY

Mendel Beiliss, a Jewish worker in Kiev, is accused of the "ritual murder" of a Christian child, unleashing a wave of anti-Semitism in Russia.

SEPTEMBER 1

Assassination of the Russian Prime Minister, Pyotr Stolypin, at the Kiev Opera House, in the presence of the Tsar and his family.

Irène Némirovsky and her mother, Anna, ca. 1912–13

1906

FEBRUARY

Irène is taken to the Carnival in Nice, France; it is her earliest memory and will inspire her to write an original screenplay in 1930.

She reads *War and Peace,* *Le Mémorial de Saint-Hélène* by Las Cases, Stendhal, Balzac, Maupassant, and Rostand. *"In those days, I was crazy about Edmond Rostand."* (Interview, Radio-Paris, June 2, 1933)

Assassination of Rasputin, "friend" of the Empress and adviser to the court.

1917

The February Revolution begins. Irène attends the mass demonstration organized by Russian women on Feburary 23, then the mock execution of Ivan, superintendent of the building in which the Némirovskys lived. *"It was on that day, at that very instant, that I saw the birth of the Revolution. I witnessed the moment when man had not quite changed his way of life or rid himself of human pity, when he was not yet possessed by the devil, but when the devil was already closing in and troubling his soul."* ("Birth of a Revolution," *Le Figaro*, June 4, 1938)

Dismissed by Irène's mother, Irène's governess, Zézelle, commits suicide by drowning herself in the Neva River. *"I don't want to call her Zézelle anymore, it's too sacred. I'll see. Mademoiselle Rose, that's good too."* (Journal, 1934/IMEC)

MARCH 20
The Provisional Government of Prince Lvov abolishes all restrictions previously imposed on the Jews.

APRIL 3
Lenin returns to Russia.

1914

The Némirovskys move to a *"rambling residence"* at 18 Angliyskiy Prospect in the Kolomna district of St. Petersburg, capital of the Russian Empire. Irène learns the piano. Leonid, now president of Voronej Commerce Bank and administrator of the Union Bank of Moscow and the Private Commerce Bank of Saint Petersburg, moves in high government circles. *"The gold streamed, the wine flowed."* (*The Wine of Solitude*, 1935)

Witnessing her mother's infidelities, Irène develops an *"abominable hatred"* of her. (*L'Ennemie*, 1928) *"In every family there is nothing but filthy greed, lying, and mutual incomprehension. It's the same everywhere. It's no different in our home. The husband, the wife, and the lover."* (*The Wine of Solitude*, 1935)

AUGUST 1
Germany declares war on Russia.

AUGUST 3
Germany declares war on France.

AUGUST 18
Saint Petersburg is renamed Petrograd.

ABOVE
Irèrne Némirovsky and her mother, Anna, n.d.

LEFT
Irène Némirovsky, ca. 1912–13

OCTOBER 25

The Bolshevik Revolution begins. The Némirovskys move to a Moscow apartment that they sublet from an officer of the Chevalier Garde. Irène reads Huysmans, Maupassant, Oscar Wilde, and Plato.

DECEMBER

The Russian banking system is declared a state monopoly.

1918

JANUARY

The Némirovskys travel by sleigh across the Finnish border to the village of Mustamäki, where they stay in a log-cabin inn with a handful of other exiles. Here Irène reads Balzac, Dumas, and Gautier. Rudolf ("Roudia"), a married man, gives Irène her first kiss and awakens within her *every exalted, poetic sensation of love."* (Journal, 1933/IMEC) She writes her first poems in Russian. *"Born among so many different people / Now I know I am a stranger here / And I could have had another destiny / The destiny to which I devote all my dreams."* (Notebook/IMEC)

APRIL

Fleeing the fighting, the Némirovskys leave for the Finnish capital of Helsinki. Irène begins reading modern French writers. In Russia, the administrative boards of the banking sector are dissolved by decree.

1919

MARCH

The Némirovskys leave Helsinki for Stockholm. *"I arrived on a winter morning of sleet mixed with snow, and a violent wind…Stockholm seemed dark, cold, sad."* (Interview, *Nord-Sud,* February 15, 1930)

LATE JUNE

Departure on a freighter at Norrköping, Sweden.

ABOVE
The Grand Hotel, Stockholm, ca. 1902

LEFT
Irène Némirovsky, ca. 1917

Arrival in Rouen, France, after a crossing of *"ten days without a stopover in a dreadful storm, which I was obliged to relive in* David Golder. *"* (Interview, *Les Nouvelles littéraires*, January 11, 1930) The Némirovskys move into a furnished apartment at 115 rue de la Pompe in Paris's 16th arrondissement. *"I had already spent time in Paris as a child. When I returned, I found memories waiting for me there."* (Interview, *Revue des deux mondes*, 1936) Irène is entrusted to the care of an English governess, Miss Matthews. She would take an immediate dislike to her *"long, horselike face."* (*L'Ennemie*, 1928) She reads Proust, Larbaud, Chardonne, Maurois, Toulet, and the Tharaud brothers.

Irène's father, Léon, rebuilds his fortune through the Paris branch of the Union Bank and the Paris-based Committee of Russian Banks in exile, under the directorship of Count Kokovtzov. Léon is falsely accused of speculating on the ruble on behalf of the Bolsheviks during his stay in Stockholm.

ABOVE
Irène Némirovsky, ca. 1919

FAR LEFT
Left to right, Miss Matthews, Irène Némirovsky, and Léon Némirovsky, ca. 1920

LEFT AND OPPOSITE
Irène Némirovsky and her father, Léon Némirovsky, n.d.

1920

FEBRUARY

Extended stay in Nice. Irène becomes friends with Olga Boutourline, the future Princess Obolensky.

NOVEMBER

The Némirovskys move into a private villa at 18 Avenue Président Wilson. Irène socializes with Paris's Russian community and becomes close friends with Alexandre "Choura" Lissianski (who would be taken in by Irène in the early 1930s), Mila Gordon, and Daria Kamenka. She enrolls at the Sorbonne to study Russian Literature, reads Merejkovski, Balmont, Kliuev, and the Russian poets of the Silver Age; she goes to the balls, nightclubs, and cabarets of Montmartre. *"I never looked down on the pleasures of youth. I traveled often and…danced a lot!"* (Interview, *Marianne*, February 13, 1935)

TOP LEFT
Irène Némirovsky, Nice, France, ca. 1920

LEFT
Alexandre "Choura" Lissianski, n.d.

1921

At the Sorbonne, Irène becomes close friends with René Avot, the son of an industrialist from Pas-de-Calais, and his sister, Madeleine ("Mad"). Excursions by car to Touquet, Deauville, Juan-les-Pins, Saint-Jean-de-Luz, Hendaye… She writes her first pieces in French, a series of "apophthegms" (aphorisms) recorded in a black notebook: *"If happiness doesn't exist, there is at least a close enough copy of it in this world—artistic creation."* (Notebook/IMEC)

AUGUST I

The humorous magazine *Fantasio* publishes one of four comic dialogues written by Irène, *Nonoche and the Clairvoyant.* → This short play was signed "Topsy," the nickname she was given by Miss Matthews. *"I was still a kid, with hair down to my shoulders and accompanied by a respectable English lady who went everywhere with me."* (Interview, *Les Nouvelles littéraires*, November 2, 1935)

SEPTEMBER

Irène enrolls at the Sorbonne for a degree in Russian Literature.

ABOVE
Irène Némirovsky, n.d.

RIGHT
Irène Némirovsky, ca. 1921

NOVEMBER
Irène is invited to spend All Saints'
Day at Lambres-lez-Douais with
Madeleine Avot.

DECEMBER
At Christmas, another stay with
the Avots. A New Year's Eve party
at the Cercle Russe, where Irène
felt *"out of place, nearly a foreigner."*
(Letter to Madeleine Avot/IMEC)

1922

Arrival in France of Irène's
maternal grandparents. →

JULY
Irène receives her degree in Russian
Literature and Language from the
Sorbonne, with honors.

SUMMER
Stay at the Hotel de la Paix in
Plombières. Brief romance with the
son of a manufacturer from Vosges.

OCTOBER 28
Enrolls for a degree in Comparative
Literature at the Sorbonne. Takes
courses from Fernand Baldensperger
and Fortunat Strowski.

1923

Irène at 20: *"She seemed to have
stopped growing and at twenty still
had the slight, fragile body of a
child that she would always have."*
(Archive Némirovsky /IMEC)
Léon rents a furnished apartment
for Irène at 24 rue Boissière; her
neighbor is the academician, poet,
and novelist Henri de Régnier
(1864–1936), who will remind her

humorously ten years later how
noisily she entertained her friends.

JULY
Trips to Deauville, Plombières,
Hendaye, Biarritz, and Vittel.

ABOVE
Jonas and Bella Margoulis,
Irène Némirovsky's maternal
grandparents, ca. 1922

LEFT
Portrait of Henri de Régnier
by Jacques-Émile Blanche

1924

MAY 9
Publication in *Le Matin* of
"La Niania" ("The Nanny"),
a precursor to *Snow in Autumn*.

JULY 10
Receives her degree from the
Sorbonne in Comparative Literature.

OCTOBER 28
France officially recognizes the
USSR. Russian exiles have until
January 1925 to claim Soviet
citizenship.

DECEMBER 31
Meets Michel Epstein at a New
Year's Eve party. *"He's courting me
and, well, I quite like him."* (Letter
to Madeleine Avot/IMEC) Born
in Moscow on October 30, 1896,
a graduate of the École des Hautes
Études in Saint Petersburg, he is the
son of the professor and financier
Efim Moisevitch Epstein,
administrator of the Bank of
Azov-Don, author of numerous
works on the Russian banking
system, and, like Léon Némirovsky,
sits on the Board of the Committee
of Russian Banks in exile. "May
what has happened to Russia,"
he wrote at the time, "serve as a
warning to the civilized world."
(*Russian Commercial Banks*, 1925)

ABOVE
Efim Moisevitch Epstein, father
of Michel Epstein, n.d.

RIGHT
Michel Epstein, ca. 1924

vient de nouveau toute une théorie
de bals, de fêtes, de soirées.

J'en ai déjà trois en perspective:
le 10, le 11, le 13 et un bal costumé
le 17. Joli?

Et puis, il y a quelque chose ou
plutôt quelqu'un me retient à
Paris. Je ne sais pas si vous
vous rappelez de Michel Epstein
un petit brun au teint très foncé
qui est revenu avec Choura et
nous en taxi par cette mémorable
nuit ou plutôt ce mémorable
matin du premier Janvier?

Letter from Irène Némirovsky to Madeleine Avot about meeting Michel Epstein,
January 1925: *"There is also something else, or should I say someone else, who is keeping
me in Paris. I don't know if you remember Michel Epstein, that short, dark-skinned
man with brown hair who came back with Choura and us in the taxi that memorable
night, or rather, memorable morning of January 1? He's courting me and, well, I quite
like him…"*

Il me fait la cour, N, ma foi,
le le trouve à mon goût. Alors,
comme le béguin est très violent
en ce moment, il ne faut pas
me demander de partir, vous
comprenez?
Je vois très souvent notre petite
bande; j'ai déjeuné plusieurs
fois avec eux; on s'est retrouvé
chez Milo pas plus tard que hier
soir et j'ai revu Bob qui m'a
demandé de tes nouvelles. Lui avez
vous écrit? Il est très discret
sur ce sujet.

1925

LATE MARCH
Michel Epstein begins working at the Banque des Pays du Nord, in charge of international transactions and the *crédits documentaires* (letters of credit) service. Irène meets him every evening at Chez Martin, Avenue George V.

SUMMER
Last vacation on the Côte Basque with her parents. *"The best time of day was at dawn, especially at the sleepy hotel: she would walk up into the hills, her hair floating down over her shoulders, wearing a blue skirt, a Lacoste blouse, in espadrilles, her arms and legs bare."* (*Le Malentendu [The Misunderstanding]*, 1926)

1926

Le Malentendu (The Misunderstanding), her first novel, appears in the monthly *Les Œuvres libres* (Fayard). It recounts the doomed love affair between an office worker and an idle rich girl. *"Ah, love is such a luxurious feeling, ma chérie…"* Irène sketches out the first draft of *David Golder*, the story of the exile and financial success of a Russian-Jewish immigrant couple, a metaphor for her own family history.

JULY 31
Michel and Irène are married in a civil ceremony in the town hall of the 16th arrondissement, preceded by a religious ceremony at the synagogue on rue Théry (today the rue de Montevideo). They move into a five-bedroom apartment on the top floor at 8 Avenue Daniel-Lesueur. Irène writes every day. *"My husband comes home. I stop working; from that moment on, I am a wife and a wife only."* (Interview, *Je suis partout*, ca. March 1935)

ABOVE
Irène Némirovsky in the French Basque country, ca. 1925

RIGHT
Michel Epstein and Irène Némirovsky, ca. 1926

Préfecture du Département de la Seine

Extrait des minutes
des Actes de Mariage

16e Arrondissement de Paris

Année 1926

DROITS D'EXPÉDITION 2.50

1.50 FRANC

Le trente-un juillet mil neuf cent vingt-six, seize heures
quinze minutes, devant Nous, Gaston ERNEST- Chevalier de la
Légion d'Honneur, adjoint au Maire du seizième arrondissement
de Paris, ont comparu publiquement en la maison commune: ****
Michel EPSTEIN, sans profession, né à Moscou (Russie), le tren
te octobre mil huit cent quatre-vingt-seize, domicilié à Paris
avenue Victor Emmanuel, III, N°29; fils de Efim EPSTEIN, et de
Elisabeth DAITZELMAN, époux sans profession, domiciliés à Paris, 29, avenue Victor Emmanuel, III, d'une part.-ET/:Irma **
Irène NEMIROVSKY, sans profession, née à Kiew (Russie), le
onze février mil neuf cent trois, domiciliée à Paris, avenue
du Président Wilson, 18; fille de Léon NEMIROVSKY, banquier,
et de Fanny Jeanne MARGOULIS, son épouse, sans profession,
domiciliés à Paris, avenue du Président Wilson, 18; d'autre
part.-Un contrat de mariage a été reçu le vingt-trois juillet
dernier par Maître GOUPIL, notaire à Paris.-Michel EPSTEIN- et
Irma Irène NEMIROVSKY, ont déclaré l'un après l'autre vouloir
se prendre pour époux, et Nous avons prononcé au nom de la Loi
qu'ils sont unis par le mariage./.

POUR EXTRAIT CONFORME.
PARIS- le douze juillet mil neuf cent trente-sept.-
LE MAIRE.

Marriage certificate of Michel
Epstein and Irène Némirovsky,
July 31, 1926

1927

L'Enfant génial (The Child Genius) appears in *Les Œuvres libres*; Némirovsky gives voice to the *"unconscious echo of the sorrowful singing of the Jews, reaching us from the very depths of time like an immense sob."*

1928

Léon ↓ becomes vice-president of the Parisian branch of the Union Bank.

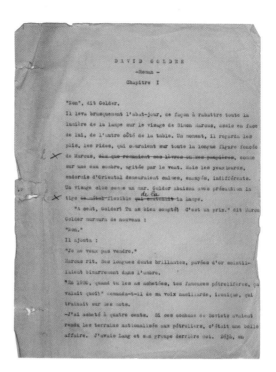

JULY

L'Ennemie (The Enemy), Irène's second novel, is published in *Les Œuvres libres* under the pseudonym Pierre Nerey, an anagram of Irène. This cruel portrait of a vain, unkind mother is the adaptation of the author's conflict with her own mother, Fanny, and the price of a solitary childhood. *"There, finally, was my vengeance…"* But *L'Ennemie* is also a satire on high society in Biarritz.

FALL

Irène returns to *David Golder*, ↑ with the help of *Oil Imperialism: The International Struggle for Petroleum* by Louis Fischer and back issues of *La Revue pétrolifère* (*Petroleum Magazine*).

1929

FEBRUARY

Le Bal (The Ball), written *"between two chapters of* David Golder," appears under the pseudonym Pierre Nerey → in *Les Œuvres libres*. Like *L'Ennemie*, it is a story of vengeance, the vengeance of a young girl abandoned by her mother, who has become rich. According to arts patron Charles de Noailles, it is "the ultimate book with a dark ending." (Jean Cocteau, *Le Passé défini*, II, September 11, 1953)

SEPTEMBER

Irène sends the manuscript of *David Golder* to André Foucault, editor-in-chief of *Les Œuvres libres*, who demands cuts.

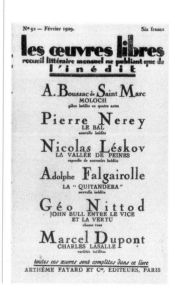

Publisher Bernard Grasset ↓ (1881–1955) places notices in the press in search of the author of *David Golder*, who submitted the manuscript under the name Epstein—most likely an advertising ploy on the part of Grasset.

NOVEMBER 9

Birth of Denise France Catherine Epstein. *"She doesn't look anything like me. She is nearly blonde, with gray eyes, but I think this will change."* (Letter to Madeleine Avot/IMEC) Cécile Mitaine enters Irène's service as a nanny. Born in Issy-l'Évêque (Saône-et-Loire) on February 24, 1904, Cécile shares Irène's birth date on the Gregorian calendar. Two or three weeks after Denise's birth, Irène goes to Grasset's offices.

TOP RIGHT
Denise Epstein and her nanny, Cécile Mitaine (later Cécile Michaud), ca.1931

RIGHT
Irène Némirovsky and her first daughter, Denise Epstein, ca. 1929

DECEMBER 7
The first copies of *David Golder* are published in the collection *"Pour mon plaisir"* ("For My Pleasure"). Bernard Grasset compares the book to Balzac's *Père Goriot* and issues a press release: "Here is a book which, in my opinion, will go very far."

1930
JANUARY 10
Writing in *Le Temps*, André Thérive sets the critical tone: "Without any doubt, *David Golder* is a masterpiece." The book enjoys stunning success. André Maurois compares its author to Proust, and Gaston de Pawlowski compares her to Tolstoy. Henri de Régnier hails "a very assured talent." (*Le Figaro*, January 28) Gaston Chérau and Roland Dorgelès sponsor Irène's candidacy for membership in the *Société des gens de lettres* (Writer's Guild).

JANUARY 11
Frédéric Lefèvre (1889–1949) conducts Irène's first interview, which appears in *Les Nouvelles littéraires* with a drawing of Irène by Jean Texcier. → "This young mother looks like a girl… Her jet-black, raven hair—as black as you can possibly imagine— is cropped like a tomboy's. Her eyes, as dark as her hair, have a strange gentleness, flashing almost imperceptibly at times, giving a hint of myopia."

FEBRUARY–MARCH
The right-wing press considers *David Golder* a satirical tract: "Only a Jew would be able to write such a frightful and clear-sighted indictment of the Jewish lust for gold." (André Billy, *La Femme de France*) Some in the "Israelite" press disparage the figure of David Golder as a "Jew for anti-Semites." (Pierre Paraf, *L'Illustration juive*) Irène Némirovsky, who acknowledges having written a social satire, defends herself with broad generalizations: *"Do the middle-class of the Marais[1] really think they can identify the unsavory types you find in a Francis Carco[2] novel? Why then do French Israelites want to see themselves in* David Golder? *The disparity is the same."* (Interview, *L'Univers israélite*, July 5, 1935) *L'Univers israélite* delivers a back-handed exoneration: "Irène Némirovsky is certainly not an anti-Semite. And neither is she Jewish." (*L'Univers israélite*, February 28, 1930)

FEBRUARY 19
Fernand Nozière (1875–1931) acquires the theatrical rights to *David Golder*. In his personal diary, the drama critic Paul Léautaud (1872–1956) said of Nozière, "He's like one of those local tailors who doesn't know how to make clothing but is happy to patch things up and finish them off. He couldn't make something of his own, something unique. He fixes up the work of others."

MARCH
Fayard re-releases *Le Malentendu (The Misunderstanding)* in its "Collection de bibliothèque."

1 Marais: Paris's historic Jewish quarter. —Trans.
2 Francis Carco: French poet and novelist (1886–1958) whose fiction often portrayed the Parisian underworld. —Trans.

MAY

For his first "talkie," filmmaker Julien Duvivier (1896–1967) undertakes an adaptation of *David Golder*. "I picked up the book one evening and couldn't put it down until I'd finished it. It is excellent." (Interview with René Jeanne and Charles Ford, Radiodifusion française, 1957)

SUMMER

Vacation at the Hotel Eskualduna in Hendaye-Plage (the Basque coast). →

AUGUST

Grasset re-releases the novella *Le Bal (The Ball)*, which he describes as the latest novel by Irène Némirovsky. Critics are disappointed by its slightness and the corruption of its heroine. Paul Reboux (1877–1963) nevertheless hails it as a "gem" and announces the arrival of a new Colette. (*Paris-Soir*, August 13, 1930)

OCTOBER

Julien Duvivier begins filming *David Golder* in the studios at Épinay-sur-Seine. The title role is played by Harry Baur (1880–1943), whom Nozière has also chosen as the lead in the stage play.

DECEMBER

Extended stay in Switzerland. In Paris, Nozière and Duvivier are at loggerheads and accuse each other of plagiarism.

DECEMBER 26

David Golder opens at the Théâtre de la Porte-Saint-Martin. The great Harry Baur, not content with shouldering the enormous role of Golder, also takes it upon himself to direct the other actors, with the "admirable intention of creating a flurry of financial investment." (*Comœdia*, December 23, 1930) Philippe Soupault (1897–1990) would call it "the most resounding failure of the year." (*L'Europe nouvelle*, March 21, 1931)

Cartoon drawn by J. Sennep depicting Paulette Andral and Harry Baur in the theatrical adaptation of Irène Némirovsky's novel *David Golder*.

1931

JANUARY 14
Jonas Margoulis dies and is buried in the Jewish section of the Père-Lachaise cemetery in Paris.

JANUARY–FEBRUARY
David Golder is serialized in *Le Peuple*, the journal of the French trade union, the CGT (*Confédération générale du travail*).

MARCH 6
World premiere of Duvivier's "great talking film" → at the Élysée Gaumont on the Champs-Élysées, attended by many celebrities, including Colette and Maurice Ravel. Paul Morand applauds "a great human journey, from the Polish ghetto to luxurious Biarritz, from rags to riches, from life to death." (*Le Figaro*, March 6, 1931) The Communist daily newspaper *L'Humanité* lambasts what it views as a defense of capitalism. The magazine *La Petite illustration* sees the film as an example of the "Jewish peril" that is threatening France. (April 11, 1931)

MARCH 18
David Golder is shown in Berlin.

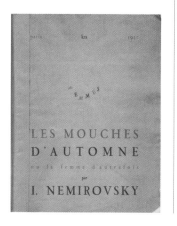

MAY
Les Mouches d'automne (Snow in Autumn) is published by Simon Kra in the collection *"Femmes"* ("Women"). ← This nostalgic tale of Russian emigration is both an expansion of the story *"La Niania"* and an intimate homage to Irène's governess, Zézelle.

Irène dreams of writing *"subjects for new films."* (*Poslednija Novosti*, n.d.).

JUNE
The Swedish tycoon Ivar Kreuger refuses to give financial assistance to Léon Némirovsky.

Irène Némirovsky (second from right) with friends in Hendaye, France, 1931.
The woman second from left is Countess Marie-Laure de Noailles.

JULY
"Film parlé" (Spoken Film), Irène's first attempt at story writing in the style of a screenplay, appears in *Les Œuvres libres*.

Vacation at the Hotel Eskualduna in Hendaye-Plage. →

SEPTEMBER 11
Adapted by Wilhelm Thiele, the musical movie version of *Le Bal (The Ball)* screens at the Gaumont-Palace. The film only does partial justice to Némirovsky's book but introduces Danielle Darrieux, a talented thirteen-year-old in her first role, as Antoinette.

SEPTEMBER 12
Irène submits a screenplay, tentatively titled *La Symphonie de Paris*, to the *Association des auteurs de films* (Screen Writer's Guild).

Michel, Irène, and daughter Denise on the beach in Hendaye, France, 1931

DECEMBER
Grasset publishes an edition of *Les Mouches d'automne (Snow in Autumn),* which is praised by critic Robert Brasillach: "Mme. Némirovsky has adapted the immense Russian melancholy into a French setting…This book, whose poetry is so moving and truthful, is sure to be read and cherished." *(Action française,* January 7, 1931)

1932

JANUARY
Extended stay in Megève, a ski resort in the Alps.

JANUARY 15
Irène submits a screenplay, titled *La Comédie bourgeoise (The Bourgeois Comedy)* to the *Association des auteurs de films* (Screen Writer's Guild).

MARCH
Extended stay in Saint-Jean-de-Luz (Pays Basque), where Michel recovers from congestion of the lungs. Irène reads *Le Nœud de vipères (Vipers' Tangle)* by François Mauriac, *"the most beautiful thing I've read in a long while."* (Letter to Pierre Tisné/Grasset Archive)

MAY 18
Death of Rosa Margoulis, who had gone almost totally blind.

MAY 21
Irène submits two screenplay projects, titled *Noël* and *Carnaval de Nice,* to the *Association des auteurs de films* (Screen Writer's Guild).

JUNE
La Comédie bourgeoise (The Bourgeois Comedy) appears in *Les Œuvres libres.*

Paul Epstein, Michel Epstein's younger brother, ca. 1926

SUMMER
Vacation in Hendaye with Michel and his brother Paul, an employee of the Lazard bank. ↑

SEPTEMBER 16
Léon Némirovsky → dies in Nice of a pulmonary embolism and is buried at the cemetery in Belleville. *"There are truly moments when we are tempted to say that heaven pushes us too far, mocks us too cruelly."* (Journal, 1934/IMEC) Financially ruined, Léon leaves his daughter an inheritance of only 600,000 francs. Fanny moves to 24 Quai de Passy (Avenue du Président Kennedy).

OCTOBER
Irène finishes a draft of *L'Affaire Courilof (The Courilof Affair),* her "terrorist" novel; it is written over the summer with the working title *Deux Hommes (Two Men). "A revolution is such a slaughterhouse! Is it really worth it? Nothing's really worth the trouble; it's true, not even life." (L'Affaire Courilof,* 1933) The film *David Golder* is released in the United States.

DECEMBER
Irène begins a new novel, *Le Pion sur l'échiquier (The Pawn on the Chessboard),* a social parable on *"the curse of work"* that is a continuation of the themes of *Le Malentendu (The Misunderstanding).* On December 30, *The Courilof Affair* is serialized in *Les Annales politiques et littéraires.*

Léon Némirovsky, n.d.

1933

JANUARY 30
Adolf Hitler becomes Chancellor of Germany.

MARCH
Irène completes a second draft of *Le Pion sur l'échiquier (The Pawn on the Chessboard)*, the story of a suicide that is also the portrait of *"the typical man of 1933,"* an office worker.

MAY
Dedicated to Michel Epstein, *The Courilof Affair* is published in book form by Grasset in the collection *"Pour mon plaisir."* The author acknowledges having been inspired by personal memories and accounts of the pre-revolutionary period in Russia, notably Leon Trotsky's *My Life*. The book was poorly received, and sales were disappointing: "We believe in our genius, stop working, and become our own victim." (*Action française*, May 25, 1933)

Irène publishes the short story *"Un Déjeuner en septembre"* ("A Lunch in September"), in the magazine *Revue de Paris*, edited by Marcel Thiébaut. Critic Robert Brasillach calls it "a masterpiece, as perfect as any story by Chekhov." (*Action française*, May 30, 1933)

SUMMER
Vacation in a rented house in Urrugne, *"a charming, ancient village"* in the mountains of the Basque country. → The house was *"an old post house during the reign of Louis XIV, with massive walls, an immense attic, and endless cupboards, stairs, and hiding-places."* (*Toute l'édition*, July 29, 1933) Irène makes an effort to recall her memories of Russia and Finland from a notebook that is a *"shapeless muddle"* which she has nicknamed *"the Monster,"* for *"there are more than enough memories and poetry in my life to make a book."* (Journal, 1933/IMEC)

Irène Némirovsky and daughter Denise in Urrugne in the French Basque country, 1933

SEPTEMBER

Irène sketches the *"poorly disguised autobiography"* that would become the novel *Le Vin de solitude (The Wine of Solitude)*, tentatively titled *La Famille Kern (The Kern Family)*. *"A real, living, red-blooded past, isn't that what every imagination deserves?"* (Journal, 1934/IMEC)

OCTOBER 24

Irène signs an exclusive twenty-year contract with the publisher Albin Michel (1873–1943) ↓ with an agreed monthly income of 4,000 francs.

OCTOBER 25

Le Pion sur l'échiquier (The Pawn on the Chessboard) is serialized in *L'Intransigeant*.

NOVEMBER 18

Thousands of the unemployed begin the first "Hunger March" from Lille to Paris.

DECEMBER 8

The story "Nativity," an adaptation of Irène's memories of Mustamäki, is published in *Gringoire*, a weekly political and literary magazine directed by Horace de Carbuccia (1891–1975). Two hundred and fifty thousand copies are printed.

CHRISTMAS

Suffering from asthma, Irène stays home alone: *"As a child, I felt I was an adult. Now, I feel old age approaching more than anything else. It's comical."* (Journal, 1933/IMEC)

1934

JANUARY–MARCH

Irène works as a drama critic for the daily newspaper *Aujourd'hui*, under the directorship of Paul Lévy. She is deeply impressed by a production of *Les Races (Race)* by Ferdinand Brückner at the Théâtre de l'Oeuvre, a chronicle of German anti-Semitism that *"revealed a terribly disturbing state of mind for the neighbors of a people for whom sadism, pride, and cruelty are so glorified."* (*Aujourd'hui*, March 10, 1934)

JANUARY–JULY

Irène writes *Le Vin de solitude (The Wine of Solitude)*, *"the story of a little girl who hates her mother."* (Journal, 1934/IMEC)

JANUARY 8

The strange "suicide" of embezzler Alexandre Stavisky, a Ukrainian Jew born in Odessa in 1886, exacerbates anti-parliamentary feeling and anti-Semitism, leading to the riots of February 6. *"One day, perhaps, I must make use of Stavisky."* (Journal, 1934/IMEC) Stavisky would indeed become the model for Daguerne in *La Proie (Prey*, 1938), and more explicitly for Ben Sinner in *Les Chiens et les Loups (Dogs and Wolves*, 1939)

FEBRUARY 6

Anti-parliamentary riots at the Place de la Concorde following the "Stavisky Affair."

MAY 16–23

The short story "Ida," a portrait of an aging actress, is published in two installments in *Marianne*, a leftist weekly journal under the directorship of Emmanuel Berl (1892–1976).

Le Pion sur l'échiquier (*The Pawn on the Chessboard*) is published by Albin Michel. Irène is not happy with it. *"I continue to depict the society I know best, composed of unbalanced people who have been displaced from the country where they would normally have lived."* (Interview, Radiodifusion française, 1934)

The critic Robert Brasillach damns *Le Pion sur l'échiquier:* "All the writer's skill isn't enough to hide the vacuity of the subject and of this book…Perhaps the author of *David Golder* shouldn't be writing novels." (*Action française*) Irène is devastated: *"Obviously I write too many books…But if they knew it was to make a living…and above all for Michel and Denise. It's hard…I am at a loss, without courage, as unhappy as can be. I feel so old!"* (Journal, 1934/IMEC)

JUNE 1

In *"Dimanche"* ("Sunday"), a short story published in the *Revue de Paris*, Irène first writes the phrase "fire in the blood" (*chaleur du sang*), which will become the title of a later novel.

JUNE 12–19

"Les Fumées du vin" ("The Vapors of Wine"), a short story composed from memories of Saint Petersburg and Finland, appears in two installments in *Le Figaro.*

SUMMER

Vacations in Hendaye and Urrugne. Irène edits *Le Vin de solitude* (*The Wine of Solitude*).

JULY 22

The short story "Echo" appears in *Noir et Blanc,* a weekly journal recently launched by Albin Michel.

OCTOBER 15

Burial of Irène's cat, Kissou, *"long, wide, shaggy, and panic-stricken."* (Interview, *Pour vous,* June 1931).

Irène Némirovsky with her cat, Kissou, Paris, ca. 1926

NOVEMBER 2

The short story *"Les Rivages heureux"* ("The Happy Shores") is published in *Gringoire*.

1935

JANUARY

Irène reads the proofs for *Le Vin de solitude*, *"which will be in the same tradition as* Le Bal.*"* (Interview, *Marianne*, February 13, 1935)

FEBRUARY

"Ida," "Film Parlé" (*Spoken Film*), *"Les Fumées du vin"* ("The Vapors of Wine"), and *"La Comédie bourgeoise"* (*The Bourgeois Comedy*) are gathered into one volume in the Gallimard collection *"Renaissance de la nouvelle"* ("Rebirth of the Short Story") edited by the diplomat and novelist Paul Morand (1888–1976) under the title *Films Parlés (Spoken Films)*. Critics are not convinced by these efforts at screenplay-style writings. →

FEBRUARY–MAY

Irène reviews literature from England (Jean Rhys), America (Pearl Buck, James M. Cain), and the Soviet Union for *La Revue hebdomadaire* (*The Weekly Review*, published by Éditions Plon). She is strongly impressed by her reading of Franz Werfel's *The Forty Days of Musa Dagh*, a novel about the Armenian genocide committed by the Ottoman Turks in 1915. It is one of the unconscious sources behind *Les Chiens et les Loups (Dogs and Wolves)*, for *"it is in a sense the story of a man who returns as a stranger among his own people and finds himself bound by ties stronger than anything he could have imagined and is thereby forced to accept the*

LA RENAISSANCE DE LA NOUVELLE

Collection dirigée par
PAUL MORAND

FILMS
parlés

par Irène Némirovsky

nrf

Septième Édition

GALLIMARD

fate of his race and of his country." (Reading notes, n.d./IMEC)

MARCH I

Le Vin de solitude (The Wine of Solitude) is serialized in the *Revue de Paris*.

APRIL I

The magazine *Revue des deux mondes* publishes the short story *"Jour d'été"* ("A Summer's Day"), a meditation on the different stages of life. Irène becomes close friends with Solange Doumic, daughter of the magazine's editor, René Doumic (1860–1937), brother-in-law of Henri de Régnier.

JUNE
Irène, Michel, and Denise move
to 10 Avenue Constant-Coquelin.

JULY 5
In an interview given to *L'Univers
israélite*, Irène acknowledges mis-
takes (*"If there had been a Hitler [at
the time], I would have greatly toned
down David Golder, and I wouldn't
have written it in the same fashion."*)
and responds to her accusers:
*"Every time I have had the opportunity,
I have declared that I am Jewish,
I have even shouted it out loud! I
am much too proud of being Jewish
to have ever dreamed of denying it."*

AUGUST
*Le Vin de solitude (The Wine of
Solitude)* is published by Albin
Michel. *"This particular novel is
one of those books that is written in
the heart and the mind long before
putting it down on paper…"*
(*Sequana*, August 1935)

SEPTEMBER 30
Irène and Michel's first daughter,
Denise Epstein, acquires
French citizenship.

OCTOBER 2
Jézabel, a novel outlined in 1934,
is serialized in the weekly journal
Marianne. The portrait of a
"monster" who refuses to grow
old and have a family, it is also
the trial of Fanny Némirovsky:
"Old, old woman, how I hate you!"

OCTOBER 25
The young critic Jean-Pierre
Maxence is dazzled by *Le Vin de
solitude (The Wine of Solitude)*
and describes it as "the point where
dream meets reality." *(Gringoire)*

NOVEMBER
With the help of René Doumic,
Irène takes the first steps in trying
to obtain French citizenship.

DECEMBER 20
The short story *"Le Commencement
et la fin"* ("The Beginning and the
End") is published in *Gringoire*.

1936
David Golder is translated
into Japanese.

JANUARY
Following a lawsuit brought against
the publisher Bernard Grasset by
his family to have him declared
mentally incompetent, Irène signs
"Hommage à Grasset" with André
Gide, Pierre Bonnard, Benjamin
Crémieux, Roger Martin du Gard,
and Jean Prévost.

↓ André Sabatier leaves Grasset and
becomes Irène's official editor at
Albin Michel and one of her most
faithful friends.

The magazine *Gringoire* offers Irène 50,000 francs for the publication of her next book, *La Proie* (*Prey*), a satire on political corruption that shows the hero's journey through life.

FEBRUARY 22
The short story *"Un Amour en danger"* ("Love in Danger") is published in *Le Figaro littéraire*, a precursor to the novel *Deux* (*Two*).

MARCH
Germany occupies the Rhineland.

MARCH 25
The short biographical narrative *"Le Mariage de Pouchkine et sa mort"* ("The Marriage and Death of Pushkin") is published in *Marianne*.

MARCH 15, APRIL 1
The short story *"Liens du sang"* ("Blood Ties") is published in *Revue des deux mondes*.

MAY
Jézabel is published by Albin Michel. *"A woman has committed murder. Why?"*

JUNE 5
Following the victory of the Popular Front, the Socialist Léon Blum (1872–1950) becomes Prime Minister. At the National Assembly, the right-wing Deputy Xavier Vallat denounces him, exclaiming, "For the first time, this ancient Gallo-Roman country will be governed by a Jew!"

SUMMER
Vacation in Urrugne. Irène hears machine-gun fire across the Spanish border. She works on *La Proie* (*Prey*).

SEPTEMBER
Irène writes the preface to the French edition of *The Postman Always Rings Twice* by James M. Cain. *"Here, no setups, no digressions, not a moment's rest. Just the* facts.[3]*"*

OCTOBER 16
Gringoire begins serialization of *La Proie* (*Prey*).

OCTOBER 31
René Doumic refuses to publish Irène's short story *"Fraternité"* on the grounds that it is "anti-Semitic." Its main character, a cultivated and refined French Jew, a product of the upper middle classes, is made brutally aware of his identity and of the danger that threatens him. *"In short, I am showing the impossibility of assimilation…I know it's true."* (Journal, 1936/IMEC)

1937

FEBRUARY 5
"Fraternité" appears in *Gringoire*, whose political editorials have anti-Semitic leanings; Irène continues to contribute to their literary pages, as she is responsible for supporting her family.

MAY 28
The short story "Epilogue" is published in *Gringoire*.

MARCH 20
Birth of Irène and Michel's second daughter, named Élisabeth after her paternal grandmother, who had died only a few weeks earlier, and Léone, in memory of her maternal grandfather. *"May God protect her. She is so dear to my heart."* (Journal, 1937/IMEC) →

SUMMER
Vacation in La Ferté-Allais, fifty kilometers from Paris. Irène works on *Deux* (*Two*), a novel first envisioned in 1934: "*Deux is the story of a naturally foolish, nasty, unstable couple who are gradually made better people by life, love, and marriage."* (Journal, 1934/IMEC)

DECEMBER 2
Death of René Doumic.

DECEMBER 6
Irène finds a notebook from her childhood in which she lists possible writing projects, notably portraits of three Jews: Blum, Stavisky, and Trotsky. For her, Blum is an example of a man who is a leader in spite of himself, a man *"for whom life is in conflict with his temperament."* (Journal, 1938/IMEC)

3 Original in English. —Trans.

1938

MARCH 11

Nazi Germany annexes Austria (the Anschluss). *"What strange times we live in…War, naturally, seems very close."* (Journal, 1938/IMEC)

SPRING

La Proie (*Prey*) is published by Albin Michel. "A Julien Sorel[4] in a time of crisis." (Advertisement)

APRIL

Irène writes a first draft of *Charlatan*, the story of the rise of an immigrant doctor who becomes a criminal out of necessity. She works on the book until August. *"It reminds me of Apollinaire's childhood, I don't know why."*

Deux (*Two*) is serialized in *Gringoire* through July 15.

APRIL 21–24

First known stay at the Hôtel des Voyageurs in Issy-l'Évêque, the village where Cécile Michaud (née Mitaine) was born, on the border of the departments of Nièvre and Saône-et-Loire. It is *"an extremely rich region, with big estates, fat animals, beautiful children. And the character of its people? How can I describe it? It's the character of all the rural farmers in the world. Tough on themselves and on others."* (*"Destinées,"* December 1940) →

MAY 26

"I must promise myself to create a Stav[isky] and not to be concerned with the effect this might have on the condition of the Jews in general… That's my task, to depict the wolves! I have no need of either herd animals or domesticated ones." (Journal, 1938/IMEC)

END OF MAY

Extended stay in Hendaye. Irène reads Kipling's memoirs.

A Russian theater troupe mounts a new production of *David Golder* at the Iéna theater. *"How could I have written such a thing?"* (Interview, *Les Nouvelles littéraires*, June 4, 1938)

JUNE 4

In *Le Figaro*, Irène publishes her recollections of Saint Petersburg in February 1917 under the title "Birth of a Revolution: Memories of a Little Girl." On the same day, she answers questions in *Les Nouvelles littéraires*: *"I have reduced my social life to a minimum. I spend nearly all my evenings at home reading and thinking."*

JUNE 25

In her work journal, Irène notes her financial problems: *"Day upon day of anxiety, the anxiety caused by money when you don't have it and yet know that you can earn it. A bitter resentment of life."* (Journal, 1938/IMEC) Her author account is 65,000 francs in the red.

SUMMER

Vacation at the Villa Ene Etchea in Hendaye. Irène reads Katherine Mansfield and rereads Proust's *In the Shadow of Young Girls in Flower* (*In Search of Lost Time*, vol. 2). The Epsteins take in a Spanish refugee. *"The house is stifling hot; the beach is stifling hot. No desire to work, and, at the same time, this vague restlessness…"* (Journal, 1938/IMEC) →

Irène begins a new novel, *Enfants de la nuit* (*Children of the Night*), *"the story of a family of Russian Jews—yes, always!—with a son who becomes Stav[isky]."* (Journal, 1938/IMEC)

OPPOSITE

Denise, Irène, Élisabeth, and Michel Epstein, Hendaye, France, 1938

ISSY-L'EVÊQUE. — Route de Luzy.

---

4 Julien Sorel: The main character in Stendhal's *The Red and the Black.* —Trans.

AUGUST 4

The short story *"Magie"* ("Magic") is published in *L'InTransigeant*. *"Somewhere in the story, among the threads that weave our destiny, there has to be a flaw, a missing stitch."*

AUGUST 5

The short story *"Nous avons été heureux"* ("We Were Happy") is published in *Marie-Claire*, the women's magazine edited by Hélène Gordon-Lazareff, the sister of Irène's friend Mila Gordon. It is the first of Irène's *"stories to earn a living."*

AUGUST 19

The short story *"Espoirs"* ("Hopes") appears in Gringoire. *"Ah, the lucky French! So calm, so happy!"*

SEPTEMBER 30

France, England, Italy, and Germany sign the Munich Agreement.

OCTOBER 15

The short story *"La Confidence"* ("The Secret") is published in the *Revue des deux mondes*.

NOVEMBER 2

The short story *"La Femme de Don Juan"* ("Don Juan's Wife") is published in the magazine *Candide*.

NOVEMBER 9

The Kristallnacht pogrom in Germany marks a brutal escalation of anti-Semitism. Dozens of Jews are murdered and hundreds more injured; hundreds of synagogues are burned; thousands of Jewish businesses and homes ransacked or destroyed; more than 25,000 Jews are deported to concentration camps.

NOVEMBER 12

In France, a government decree makes it more difficult for foreigners to be granted French nationality and the situation for "undesirables" worsens.

NOVEMBER 23

The Epsteins submit a new request for naturalization to the prefecture of police. Despite recommendations from prestigious individuals—Jean Vignaud, president of the Writer's Guild, and André Chaumeix, the new director of the *Revue des deux mondes*—the request is denied.

DECEMBER

Irène and Michel Epstein take steps toward converting to Catholicism. On December 21, on the advice of Father Roger Bréchard, whom they had met in Auvergne, Irène writes to Monseigneur Vladimir Ghika ↑ (1873–1954), a Romanian bishop who is well known in the Parisian literary world and a minister to the poor in the "Communist zone" of Villejuif, a southern suburb of Paris with a Communist local government.

1939

JANUARY 4–MARCH 15

Irène delivers a series of six lectures on Radio-Paris with the theme "Great Foreign Female Novelists."

JANUARY 24

Irène finds inspiration for the final title of the novel in progress she had called *Enfants de la nuit* (*Children of the Night*): *"Dogs and wolves caught between darkness and the fires of hell."* (Journal, 1939/IMEC)

FEBRUARY 2

Irène and Michel and their two daughters are baptized by Monseigneur Ghika at the chapel of Sainte-Marie Abbey in Paris's 16th arrondissement, with Father Bréchard as godfather to the children. On March 25 Irène would write in a letter to Monseigneur Ghika, *"The Catholic Church has truly found a very poor recruit in me."*

FEBRUARY 17

In *Je suis partout*, the fascist and anti-Semitic newspaper he edited at the time, Robert Brasillach calls for stripping "all Jews, half-Jews, and quarter-Jews" of French nationality.

MARCH

Michel is gravely ill with pneumonia, and nearly dies. *"Don't forget me, Monseigneur, for I am very angry, with others and with myself, and very discouraged, and only your blessing can help me through."* (Letter to Monseigneur Ghika, March 25, 1939)

The novel *Deux* (*Two*) is published in book form and advertised as Irène Némirovsky's "first love story." It is favorably received by critics and the public alike and becomes her novel that sells the most copies since *David Golder*.

MARCH 15
German troops invade Czechoslovakia and occupy the Sudetenland.

APRIL 21
An amendment is made to the Marchandeau Law of 1939 that outlaws racist and anti-Semitic attacks in the press.

APRIL 27
Michel Epstein slowly begins to recover. *"I was so afraid of losing him. I don't know what I would have done without the great good fortune of appealing to God with trust and hope."* (Letter to Monseigneur Ghika, 1939)

MAY 18–AUGUST 24
Charlatan, renamed *Les Échelles du Levant* (*The Ports of the Levantine*) is published serially in *Gringoire*. This novel about immigration appeared in France in 2005 under the title *Le Maître des âmes* (*Master of Souls*): *"Yes, all you who despise me, you rich, happy French, what I wanted was your culture, your morality, your virtues, everything that is better than me, different from me, different from the filth where I was born!"*

TOP LEFT
Irène Némirovsky, ca. late 1930s

LEFT
Irène Némirovsky's 1939 annual membership card for the Rodin Museum, Paris.

AUGUST 23
The German-Soviet Nonaggression Pact is signed. In Hendaye, the Epsteins savor the last hours of peace.

SEPTEMBER 1
German troops invade Poland. Jean Vignaud tries to push forward the naturalization process for the Epsteins, but it is in vain.

SEPTEMBER 3
France and England declare war on Germany. As a precaution, Denise and Élisabeth Epstein are sent to live in Issy-l'Évêque with Mme. Mitaine, the mother of their nanny, Cécile Michaud. Irène travels frequently between Paris and Issy up until May 1940.

OCTOBER–DECEMBER
Irène publishes articles in the foreign press and gives radio talks praising the courage of the French.

OCTOBER 5
The short story *"La Nuit en wagon"* ("The Night on the Train") is published in *Gringoire*. *"You wouldn't think we were at war."*

OCTOBER 11
Les Chiens et les Loups (*Dogs and Wolves*) begins to be serialized in *Candide*, a weekly magazine from the Fayard publishing house with a circulation of 400,000.

Irène, Élisabeth, and Denise Epstein, Hendaye, France, 1939

OCTOBER 27

The short story *"Comme des grands enfants"* ("Like Big Children") is published in *Marie-Claire*.

NOVEMBER

Irène writes the short story *"En raison des circonstances"* ("Under the Circumstances"), a preliminary sketch for the novel *Les Feux de l'automne (The Fires of Autumn)*. She begins writing her *La Vie de Tchekhov (The Life of Chekhov)*.

NOVEMBER 10

Death of Efim Epstein, Michel's father.

NOVEMBER 30

The Soviet Union marches into Finland, launching the "Winter War."

DECEMBER 7

The short story *"Le Spectateur"* ("The Spectator") is published in *Gringoire*. *"We saw a country shudder and die while singing, the way the beating heart of a wounded nightingale would feel in our hands."*

1940

JANUARY 1

The *Revue des deux mondes* publishes "Aïno," a short story inspired by memories of the 1918 civil war in Finland.

FEBRUARY 1

In *"Le Sortilège"* ("The Spell"), the narrator, named Irène, evokes childhood memories of a dacha on the outskirts of Kiev.

Travel document for Irène Némirovsky, dated December 21, 1939, giving her permission to travel by train from Paris to Issy-l'Évêque for the purpose of "seeing her children."

FEBRUARY 2

The short story *"…et je l'aime encore"* ("And I Still Love Him…") is published in *Marie-Claire*.

EARLY MARCH

Extended stay in Issy-l'Évêque. → Irène begins a new novel, *Jeunes et Vieux (The Young and the Old)*, the chronicle of a French family between the wars modeled on Noel Coward's *Cavalcade*. *"In short, my girl, you want to write your own little* War and Peace*!"* (Journal, 1940/IMEC)

EARLY APRIL

Another stay in Issy-l'Évêque. Élisabeth has scarlet fever. *Les Chiens et les Loups (Dogs and Wolves)* is published. *"This novel is a story about Jews. More specifically, not about French Jews but Jews who come from the East, Ukraine or Poland…I believe that certain Jews will recognize themselves in my characters. Will they perhaps hold it against me? But I know I speak the truth."* This novel will receive very little attention in the press.

ABOVE RIGHT
Irène Némirovsky and daughter Élisabeth, Issy-l'Évêque, 1940

RIGHT
Travel document for Michel Epstein, dated April 23, 1940, giving him permission to travel by train from Paris to Issy-l'Évêque for the purpose of "seeing his children."

APRIL 11
The short story *"Le Départ pour la fête"* ("Going to the Celebration") is published in *Gringoire*.

MAY
"La Jeunesse de Tchekhov" ("The Early Life of Chekhov"), an excerpt from *La Vie de Tchekhov* (*The Life of Chekhov*), is published in *Les Œuvres libres*.

MAY 3
The short story *"L'Autre jeune fille"* ("The Other Young Girl") is published in *Marie-Claire*.

MAY 10
German troops launch an offensive on the western front. The battle for France begins. Irène moves to Issy-l'Évêque.

JUNE 10
Michel, very weak from his illness, leaves his post at the bank and goes to Orléans.

JUNE 14
German troops march down the Champs-Élysées. At Issy-l'Évêque, Irène witnesses the mass exodus of the French toward the south of the country. On June 26, Denise would write: "From Friday to Tuesday, we watched thousands of cars pass through our usually quite tranquil area driven by people running away from the enemy."

JUNE 21
German soldiers arrive in Issy-l'Évêque.

JUNE 22
Maréchal Philippe Pétain (1856–1951), the new French Head of State who had enjoyed immense popularity following the Battle of Verdun in 1917, signs an armistice with Germany. A line of demarcation is established that separates the "unoccupied zone" in the south from the "occupied zone" in the north, which includes the town of Issy-l'Évêque.

JUNE 25
A radio broadcast by Maréchal Pétain announces, "A new era of stability has begun."

JULY 1
The Albin Michel publishing house reopens under the directorship of Robert Esménard, the publisher's son-in-law.

JULY 10
A new constitution abolishes the Third Republic, setting up a "French State" and virtually conferring absolute power on Maréchal Pétain; the new government's headquarters are in the resort town of Vichy.

MID-AUGUST
Dismissed from the Banque des Pays du Nord for leaving his post, Michel Epstein receives 8,027 francs in compensation.

AUGUST 27
The Marchandeau Law is rescinded. Racist and anti-Semitic writings in the press are legal.

AUGUST 28
The short story "Monsieur Rose" is published in *Candide*. A variation of this character would become the porcelain collector Charles Langelet in *Suite Française*.

SEPTEMBER 13
Anxious about measures announced against "stateless" people, Irène writes to Maréchal Pétain: *"I am unable to believe, Monsieur le Maréchal, that no distinction whatsoever can be made between undesirables and those honorable foreigners who have received royal hospitality from France but have conscientiously made every effort to deserve it."*

OCTOBER 3
The "Jewish Laws" are published, excluding Jews from civil service, the press, education, and the performing arts, and making them liable to be interned in "special camps."

OCTOBER 4
Irène Némirovsky's name does not appear on the "Otto List" of banned Jewish authors. Robert Esménard plans to publish *La Vie de Tchekhov* (*The Life of Chekhov*).

OCTOBER 7

Irène and Michel Epstein → are listed as Jews in the census of the sub-prefecture of Autun, which includes Issy-l'Évêque.

OCTOBER 8

Jean Fayard breaks the contract committing him to publish *Jeunes et Vieux (The Young and the Old)* in the magazine *Candide* under the final title of *Les Biens de ce monde (All Our Worldly Goods)*.

OCTOBER 22

Irène learns of the death of Father Bréchard in the Vosges on June 20 of a gunshot wound to the head. He would become the model for the character of Philippe Péricand in *Suite Française*.

OCTOBER 24

Maréchal Pétain meets Hitler in Montoire, the beginning of political "collaboration" with Germany.

OCTOBER 29

Irène decides to publish under a pseudonym. *"At times, unbearable anxiety. The feeling of being in a nightmare. No faith in reality. Faint, absurd hope."* (Journal, 1940/IMEC)

NOVEMBER

Irène envisages a novel about the Fall of France and the mass exodus of June 1940, tentatively titled *Panique (Panic)* or *Tempête (Storm)*, on the model of Louis Bromfield's *The Rains Came: A Novel of Modern India* (1937). *"How amusing this would be! At the rate things are going, it would be a posthumous work, but still."* (Journal, 1940/IMEC) Irène re-reads Tolstoy, Pushkin, and Lord Byron.

DECEMBER

The short stories *"La Peur"* ("Fear") and *"Les Cartes"* ("The Playing Cards"), signed "C. Michaud," are turned down by the weekly magazine *Aujourd'hui*.

DECEMBER 5

Under the pseudonym Pierre Nérey, Irène publishes the short story *"Destinées"* ("Destinies") in the magazine *Gringoire*, which had become openly anti-Semitic and supportive of Maréchal Pétain, and where she feels *"like someone who makes fine lace in the midst of savages."* (Journal 1940/IMEC)

DECEMBER 11
André Sabatier returns from a
trip to Syria and convinces Robert
Esménard of Albin Michel to
continue making monthly advances
to Irène in 1941, despite the
deficit in her author's account.

1941

MARCH

Fayard publishes Colette's memoir *Looking Backwards*. *"If that's all she was able to get out of June [1940], I'm happy."* (Journal, 1941/IMEC)

MARCH 20

The short story *"La Confidente"* is published in *Gringoire* under the pseudonym Pierre Nérey.

MARCH 29

A Commission for Jewish Questions is established under the direction of Xavier Vallat.

SPRING

Irène drafts the short stories *"L'Inconnu"* ("The Unknown"), under the pseudonym C. Michaud, and *"La Voleuse"* ("The Thief").

APRIL 2

Irène completes the first draft of *Tempête en Juin (Storm in June)*.

APRIL 10–JUNE 20

Les Biens de ce monde (All Our Worldly Goods), publicized as "an unpublished novel by a young woman," is serialized in *Gringoire*.

APRIL 26

Bank accounts owned by Jews are frozen.

MAY 30

The short story *"L'Honnête Homme"* ("The Honest Man") is published in *Gringoire* under the pseudonym Pierre Nérey.

JUNE 2

A second set of "Jewish Laws" is enacted. More restrictive than the first, they include a list of prohibited occupations for Jews.

JUNE 21

The Germans in Issy-l'Évêque celebrate the first anniversary of their arrival at the Château de Montrifaut, owned by the Marquis de Villette, who was the model for the Comte de Montmort in *Suite Française*. ↑

JUNE 22

German forces invade the Soviet Union, launching Operation Barbarossa, the code name given to the invasion by the Nazis. Fearful of being arrested, Irène engages Julienne ("Julie") Dumot, who formerly worked for Léon Némirovsky and, prior to that, for Sacha Guitry and Tristan Bernard. She is to care for Denise and Élisabeth and be used as a "front person" for Irène. Irène deposits a will with a notary in Issy-l'Évêque that gives Dumot legal guardianship of the children and authorizes her, *"if worst comes to worst,"* to publish *"a novel I may not have the time to finish called* Storm in June.*"*

JUNE 28

Departure of the German troops stationed at Issy-l'Évêque. *"I feel sorry for these poor young men. But I can't forgive certain people, whom I revile, those who coldly leave us to die…"* (Journal, 1941/IMEC)

JULY

The mayor of Issy-l'Évêque is relieved of his duties and replaced by the Marquis de Villette. Julie Dumot arrives on July 11. Irène works on a second draft of *Storm in June* and begins *Dolce*, part two of *Suite Française*. It is the story of the occupation of Issy-l'Évêque and a critique of the *"hive mentality"*—nationalism and the idea of *"communal destiny."* Simultaneously, she starts to work on a short novel, *Chaleur du sang (Fire in the Blood)*, a parable about the different stages of life and set in the region of Issy-l'Évêque.

AUGUST 8

The short story *"L'Inconnu"* ("The Unknown") appears in *Gringoire*. This pacifist fable includes a German soldier named Hohmann, like the lieutenant with whom Michel had become friends.

SEPTEMBER 2

Michel writes to the sub-prefecture of Autun requesting permission to travel to Paris.

SEPTEMBER 5

The short story *"Les Revenants"* ("Ghosts") appears in *Gringoire* under the pseudonym Pierre Nérey. *"How strange we really are! Our weak memory preserves only a trace of happiness, so deeply engrained that it is almost a wound."*

SEPTEMBER 19

Fall of Kiev. In Ukraine, the *Einsatzgruppen*—paramilitary groups organized by Heinrich Himmler and operated by the SS—begin the massive, systematic murder of Jewish populations.

OCTOBER

The Gibé film company hopes to adapt *Les Biens de ce monde* (*All Our Worldly Goods*) for the screen. *"This proves…that a known author isn't always necessary for a work to be successful."* (Letter to André Sabatier/IMEC)

OCTOBER 24

The short story *"L'Ogresse"* ("The Ogress") is published in *Gringoire* under the pseudonym Charles Blancat.

NOVEMBER 11

The Epsteins and Julie Dumot move into a house with a kitchen garden and an orchard. Irène begins work on a new novel, *Les Feux de l'automne* (*The Fires of Autumn*), in the vein of *All Our Worldly Goods* but more pessimistic.

DECEMBER 1

In anticipation of a trip to Paris, Irène retrieves manuscripts she had deposited with the notary in Issy-l'Évêque, including those for *David Golder*.

DECEMBER 17

Julie Dumot signs an author contract with Albin Michel for two novels by Irène Némirovsky, including *Les Biens de ce monde* (*All Our Worldly Goods*).

CHRISTMAS

Denise and Élisabeth spend the holidays with Julie Dumot in Cézac in southwestern France.

1942

FEBRUARY

Deux (*Two*) and *Les Chiens et les Loups* (*Dogs and Wolves*) are reprinted "by special permission." Robert Esménard prepares the proofs for *La Vie de Tchekhov* (*The Life of Chekhov*).

Irène writes to the *Kreiskommandantur* in Autun to request permission to travel to Paris for the purpose of seeing her publisher and having Denise examined by an ophthalmologist. Bernard Grasset refuses her any assistance, so she appeals for help as well from Hélène Morand, wife of Paul Morand.

FEBRUARY 22

"L'Incendie" ("The Fire") is published in *Gringoire* under the pseudonym Pierre Nérey; it is the last of Irène's short stories to appear in the magazine. Its editor, Horace de Carbuccia, will no longer publish *Tempête en juin* (*Storm in June*), for which Irène was expecting 50,000 francs. Her account at Albin Michel has a negative balance of 120,000 francs. Michel Epstein stops paying rent for the family's apartment in Paris.

MARCH

Rereading her notes from April 1940 regarding the composition of *Les Biens de ce monde* (*All Our Worldly Goods*), Irène is taken aback to realize that she had felt a *"sincere, slightly mocking affection"* for the French. Taking care to note the date, she adds above that sentence: *"hatred + contempt = March 1942."* (Journal, 1942/IMEC) In the margin of the manuscript for *Dolce* she records these notes on the "State of France": *"My God! What is this country doing to me? Since it is rejecting me, let us consider it coldly, let us watch as it loses its honor and its life."*

Irène begins drafting *Captivité* (*Captivity*),[5] which she also calls *Servage* (*Bondage*), the third section of *"the series Tempêtes [Storms]"*: *"As for me, I'm working on burning hot lava."* (Notes on *Captivity*, 1942/IMEC)

APRIL 1–3

André Sabatier visits Issy-l'Évêque.

5 See pages 145–56 in the present volume.

APRIL 9–11

Denise is sent to Paris with Julie Dumot to consult an ophthalmologist and collect her belongings from the Paris apartment. She then goes to Audenge in the Arcachon basin, where she stays until the end of May.

APRIL 16

President Pierre Laval (1883–1945), the champion of collaboration who was on the sidelines in December 1940, is returned to power.

APRIL 24

"A suite must be made of Tempête, Dolce, *and* Captivité.*"* The subject of this *"Suite française"* will be the *"struggle between individual and communal destiny."* ("Notes on the State of France," 1942/IMEC)

MAY 4

In a letter to André Sabatier, Irène considers *Suite française "the most important work"* of her life.

MAY 17

Irène presses André Sabatier to publish *Les Feux de l'automne (The Fires of Autumn)*. Horace de Carbuccia's reluctance is the last straw for her *"state of bitterness, weariness, and disgust."* (Letter to André Sabatier, 1942/IMEC)

MAY 29

Jews are required to wear the yellow star. Only Élisabeth, who is under six years old, is exempt. "Mama told me that I was Jewish on the day we were required to wear the yellow star." (Denise Epstein, quoted in "Les filles d'Irène Némirovsky," by Myriam Anissimov, *Les Nouveaux cahiers*, spring 1992)

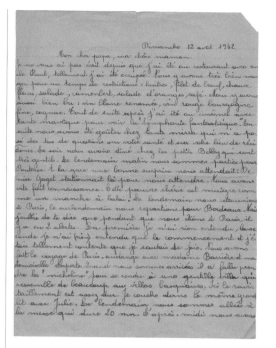

JUNE?

Irène writes the short story *"La Grande Allée"* ("The Wide Avenue").

JUNE 17

Seventeen of the twenty-two chapters of *Dolce* are finished. Irène imagines the fate of her characters in *Captivité (Captivity)*, as well as in two more planned sections, *Batailles (Battles)* and

La Paix (Peace), which would see the *"triumph of individual destiny."* The ensemble would form *"a thick volume of a thousand pages."* ("Notes on the State of France," 1942/IMEC)

ABOVE

Letter from Denise Epstein to her parents, Sunday, April 12, 1942, while traveling to Paris and Audenge with her nanny, Julie Dumot. "My dear papa, my dear mama, I haven't written to you since I went to the restaurant with Uncle Paul, that's how busy I've been. Considering there are such shortages of food, we had a really good meal: oysters, beef tenderloin, cauliflower, salad, camembert, a salad of oranges, coffee....After that we went to the movies with Aunt Mavlik to see "Symphonie Fantastique." Then we went for a snack at Aunt Mira's, who asked me lots of questions about your health, the place where you live…"

JULY 1

In Paris, Theodor Dannecker and Adolf Eichmann plan the imminent departure of the first six convoys of a thousand French Jews bound for the Nazi death camp of Auschwitz-Birkenau.

JULY 8

A second "Otto List" requires that "all books by Jewish authors" be removed from bookshops. A German edict prohibits Jews from going to theaters or any other public places.

JULY 11

"I have written a lot recently. I suppose that these will be posthumous works, but it makes the time pass more quickly." (Letter to André Sabatier, 1942/IMEC) →

JULY 13

Irène Némirovsky is arrested at her home in Issy-l'Évêque in the morning and taken to the police station at Toulon-sur-Arroux, on the pretext of "the general laws against stateless Jews between the ages of sixteen and forty-five." In fact, she had been denounced.

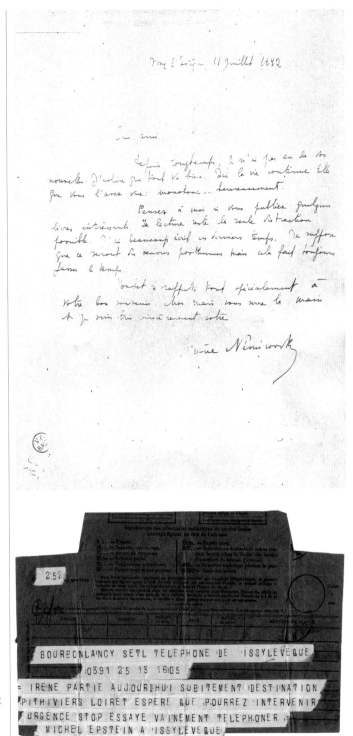

RIGHT

Telegram sent by Michel Epstein to Robert Esménard and André Sabatier on the day of Irène Némirovsky's arrest: "IRENE LEFT SUDDENLY TODAY DESTINATION PITHIVIERS LOIRET HOPE YOU CAN INTERCEDE URGENT STOP TRY TO TELEPHONE NO SUCCESS MICHEL EPSTEIN ISSY-L'EVEQUE"

JULY 15
Irène arrives at the Pithiviers internment camp ↑ in the Loiret region of France. Her last short story published in her lifetime, *"Les Vierges"* ("The Virgins") appears in the weekly "maréchaliste" magazine *Présent* under the pseudonym Denise Mérande: *"Look at me. I am alone like you now, but I have not sought or chosen solitude; mine is the worst kind of solitude, formed of bitterness and humiliation, the result of having been abandoned, betrayed."*

JULY 16
"Epstein Irène Némirovski, woman of letters" is registered at the Pithiviers camp. Irène writes a last letter to her husband and daughters: *"My dearest love, my cherished children, I think we are leaving today. Courage and hope. You are in my heart, my loved ones. May God help us all."* ↓

JULY 16–17
In Paris, more than 13,000 Jews are rounded up and assembled in the Vélodrome d'Hivers[6] to await deportation. Among them is Michel's brother, Paul Epstein.

JULY 17
At 6:15 AM, convoy number six departs from Pithiviers for Auschwitz-Birkenau with 809 men and 119 women.

JULY 19
Convoy number six arrives at Auschwitz-Birkenau at approximately 7:00 PM.

JULY 24
Samuel Epstein, older brother of Michel and Paul, and his wife, Alexandra, are deported to Auschwitz-Birkenau. →

6 Vélodrome d'Hivers: A cycling stadium near the Eiffel Tower. —Trans.

JULY 27
Despairing of help from Hélène Morand and Secretary of State Jacques Benoist-Méchin, Michel drafts a letter to Otto Abetz, German Ambassador to occupied France, pleading Irène's cause. Realizing the great risk involved to all concerned, André Sabatier decides not to deliver the letter.

AUGUST 9
Michel learns that the prisoners at Pithiviers were taken "to the East—probably Poland or Russia." Hélène Morand suggests that he appeal to the Union Générale des Israélites de France (UGIF).

AUGUST 12
André Sabatier writes to Michel, "Alas! I have done all that I am able to do."

AUGUST 19
Irène Némirovsky dies of typhus; the time was 3:20 PM according to the official Auschwitz document, which mentions the "flu."

Cher Ami,

Je viens d'apprendre, d'une source très sérieuse, que les femmes (les hommes aussi d'ailleurs, et les enfants) internées dans le camp de Pithiviers ont été conduites à la frontière d'Allemagne et de là dirigées vers l'Est - Pologne ou Russie probablement. Ceci se serait passé il y a environ 3 semaines.

Jusqu'à maintenant, je croyais ma femme dans un camp quelconque en France, sous la garde de soldats français. Savoir qu'elle se trouve dans un pays sauvage, dans des conditions probablement atroces, sans argent ni vivres et parmi des gens dont elle ne connaît même pas la langue, c'est intolérable. Il ne s'agit plus maintenant d'essayer de la faire sortir plus ou moins rapidement d'un camp, mais de lui sauver la vie.?

Vous devez avoir reçu mon télégramme d'hier; je vous ai signalé un livre de ma femme, "Les Mouches d'Automne", paru d'abord chez Kra, en édition de luxe, et ensuite chez Grasset. Ce livre est nettement antibolchévique, et je suis désolé de ne pas y avoir pensé plus tôt. J'espère qu'il n'est pas trop tard pour insister, cette nouvelle preuve en mains, auprès des autorités allemandes.

Je sais, cher ami, que vous faites tout ce que vous pouvez pour nous sauver, mais je vous en supplie, trouvez, imaginez encore autre chose, consultez de nouveau Morand, Chambrun, votre ami et, plus particulièrement, le Docteur BAZY, Président de la Croix Rouge Française, 12, Rue Newton, Tél. KLE 84-05 (le Chef de son secrétariat particulier est Mme ROUSSEAU, même adresse) en leur signalant ce nouveau motif que sont "Les Mouches d'Automne". Il est tout de même inconcevable que nous, qui avons tout perdu à cause des Bolcheviks, nous soyons condamnés à mort par ceux qui les combattent!

Enfin, cher ami, c'est un dernier appel que je lance. Je sais que je suis impardonnable d'abuser ainsi de vous et des amis qui nous restent encore, mais, je le répète, c'est une question de vie ou de mort non seulement pour ma femme, mais aussi pour nos enfants, sans parler de moi-même. C'est sérieux. Seul ici, avec les gosses, presqu'en prison puisqu'il m'est interdit de bouger, je n'ai même pas la consolation d'agir. Je ne peux plus ni dormir, ni manger: que cela serve d'excuse à cette lettre incohérente.

Bien à vous.

Letter from Michel Epstein to André Sabatier, August 9, 1942: "I have just learned, from a very reliable source, that the women (and men and even the children) interned at the Pithiviers camp were taken to the German border and from there sent to the East—probably Poland or Russia.... Until now, I thought my wife was in some camp in France, in the custody of French soldiers. To learn she is in an uncivilized country, in conditions that are probably atrocious, without money or food and with people whose language she does not even know, is unbearable. It is now no longer a matter of getting her out of a camp sooner rather than later, but of saving her life.... I know, dear friend, that you are doing everything you can to save us, but I beg of you, find, think of something else, speak again to Morand, Chambrun, your friend and in particular to Dr. Bazy, President of the French Red Cross . . . Alas, dear friend, I am launching one final appeal. I know that it is unforgivable to impose on you and the rest of our remaining friends in this way, but, I say it again, it is a question of life and death not only for my wife, but also for our children, not to mention myself. It's serious. Alone here, with the little ones, virtually imprisoned since it is forbidden for me to move, I don't even have the consolation of being able to act. I can no longer either sleep or eat: please accept that as an excuse for this incoherent letter. Yours . . ."

8. 10. 42

Merci mille fois, chère
Madame, pour toute la
peine que vous vous donnez.
N'abandonnez pas les
petites, si un malheur
leur arrive. Je suis
sûr que vous faites
tout ce que vous pouvez
pour sauver Irène.
Continuez, je vous en
supplie.
        Bien à vous

* Mes très sincères remerciements
à M. Aust. Ma femme et
aimait beaucoup

OCTOBER 8

Michel Epstein confers all authority over his daughters to Julie Dumot and writes to Madeleine Avot-Cabour, "Don't abandon the little ones if some misfortune befalls them." ←

OCTOBER 9

Michel is arrested and taken to the police prefecture at Autun. Denise and Élisabeth are spared, and he entrusts to them the suitcase containing *Suite Française*. He is taken to Le Creusot prison, then to the transit camp at Drancy near Paris. ↑

END OF OCTOBER

Two policemen and a member of the Milice (the infamous French paramilitary corps that worked for the Nazis) go to the school in Issy-l'Évêque to arrest Denise and Élisabeth, but they are hidden and flee to Bordeaux with Julie Dumot.

NOVEMBER 6

Convoy number forty-two leaves Drancy for Auschwitz-Birkenau. All of its occupants are gassed upon arrival; among them is Michel Epstein.

1943

Denise and Élisabeth are hidden under false names in a Catholic boarding school, then, after February 1944, with a family.

FEBRUARY 23

The short story *"Un beau mariage"* ("A Happy Marriage"), rejected by *Gringoire* in December 1941, is published in *Présent* with the author's name given as Denise Mérande.

1944

AUGUST 24

Paris is liberated.

AUGUST 28

Bordeaux is liberated.

1945

JANUARY

The Auschwitz-Birkenau death camp is "liberated" by the Soviets.

FEBRUARY

The French Ministry of Prisoners, Deportees, and Refugees is unable to obtain information about the fate of the writers Benjamin Crémieux, Robert Desnos, Irène Némirovsky…

MAY 7

The Armistice is signed at Reims. Deportees gradually begin to return. A Family Panel is established consisting of the Banque des Pays du Nord, the Writer's Guild, and the publisher Albin Michel to provide for the education of Irène Némirovsky's daughters until they reach their legal majority. Élisabeth is placed with the Avot family, and Denise is sent to a Catholic boarding school.

1946

JULY

"La Mort de Tchekhov" ("The Death of Chekhov"), an excerpt from *La Vie de Tchekhov* (*The Life of Chekhov*), appears in *La Nef.*

OCTOBER

La Vie de Tchekhov (*The Life of Chekhov*) ↓ is published by Albin Michel, with a preface by Jean-Jacques Bernard (son of Tristan Bernard), who was himself a survivor of Compiègne, the "camp of slow death." "Born in the East, Irène was taken to die in the East. Uprooted from life in her native land, she was again uprooted and sent to die by the country she had chosen as her own. Between these two chapters she led a life that was too short, but brilliant: a young Russian girl came and wrote in the golden book of our language words that enrich it. Because of the twenty years she spent with us, we mourn her as a French writer."

1947

FEBRUARY

Les Biens de ce monde (*All Our Worldly Goods*) is published by Albin Michel.

1957

Les Feux de l'automne (*The Fires of Autmn)* is published by Albin Michel.

1972

Fanny Némirovsky dies and is buried in the Jewish section of the Belleville cemetery. Her granddaughters discover a copy of *Jézabel* and *David Golder* in her safe.

1988

Irène Némirovsky's maternal aunt, Victoria, dies in Moscow.

3ᵉ Mille

IRÈNE NÉMIROVSKY

LA VIE
DE
TCHEKOV

Avant-Propos de
JEAN-JACQUES BERNARD

ÉDITIONS
ALBIN MICHEL

MINISTERE
DES
ANCIENS COMBATTANTS
ET
VICTIMES DE GUERRE

REPUBLIQUE FRANÇAISE

M. 8 bis.

DIRECTION DU CONTENTIEUX
DE L'ETAT-CIVIL
ET DES RECHERCHES

Paris, le ....18.OCT..1946

139, rue de Bercy
PARIS 12°

ACTE DE DISPARITION

LE MINISTRE DES ANCIENS COMBATTANTS
ET VICTIMES DE GUERRE,

Vu l'article 88 du Code Civil (Ord. du 30 octobre 1945) ;

Après examen des pièces du dossier portant le n° .20..841

DECLARE :

DUPLICATA

la disparition de E P S T E I N née N E M I R O W S K Y Irma Irène

né le .II Février 1903 à .KIEW (Russie)

dans les conditions indiquées ci-après :

- Arrêtée le I3 Juillet 1942 à ISSY-L'EVEQUE.
- Internée le 16 Juillet 1942 à PITHIVIERS.
- Déportée le 17 Juillet 1942 à AUSCHWITZ (Pologne).

Pour le Ministre des Anciens Combattants
et Victimes de Guerre,
Par délégation, le Directeur du Contentieux,
de l'Etat-civil et des Recherches.

P. O.

REMARQUES IMPORTANTES

1° Cet acte de disparition n'est pas un acte de décès, il ne doit pas être transcrit sur le registre des actes de décès de la mairie.

2° La famille ne doit pas se dessaisir de cet acte. En cas de besoin pour faire valoir ses droits, elle établit une copie qu'elle fait certifier conforme par le maire ou le commissaire de police.

3° La famille peut demander :

— soit un jugement déclaratif de décès, par simple lettre adressée au Procureur de la République du domicile du disparu, sans ministère d'avoué et sans frais, en application de la loi du 30 avril 1946, si le disparu est de nationalité française et appartient à l'une des catégories suivantes : Mobilisé, Prisonnier de guerre, Réfugié, Déporté ou Interné politique, Membre des Forces françaises libres ou des Forces françaises de l'intérieur, Requis du service du travail obligatoire ou Réfractaire.

— soit un jugement déclaratif d'absence (ou de décès si un délai de 5 ans s'est écoulé depuis le jour de la disparition) en application de la loi du 22 septembre 1942 validée et modifiée par l'Ordonnance d'Alger du 5 avril 1944.

D'autre part, à tout moment, l'acte de disparition peut être transformé par la Direction du contentieux, de l'Etat-civil et des Recherches en acte de décès si les preuves du décès sont apportées.

A.C.V.G. — Réaumur, 21.903.

Death certificate for Irène Némirovsky issued by the French government on October 18, 1946.

1992

APRIL

Le Mirador, mémoires rêvés (The Watchtower: An Imaginary Memoir) is published by Presses de la Renaissance. It is a fictional biography of Irène Némirovsky by her daughter, Élisabeth Gille (née Epstein), and is awarded the WIZO Book Award for French writers.

1995

SEPTEMBER 30

Élisabeth Gille and Denise Epstein entrust the Irène Némirovsky archive to IMEC.

1996

SEPTEMBER 30

Death of Élisabeth Gille, writer, translator, and editor. In the same year, Éditions du Seuil publishes *Un Paysage de cendres (A Landscape of Ashes)*, a novel about her childhood as an orphan.

2000

MARCH

A collection of fifteen short stories by Irène Némirovsky, *Dimanche, et autres nouvelles (Sunday and Other Stories)*, is published by Éditions Stock.

2004

APRIL

A collection of thirteen short stories by Irène Némirovsky, *Destinées, et autres nouvelles (Destinies and Other Stories)*, is published by Sables.

NOVEMBER 8

Suite Française is published by Denoël and wins the Prix Renaudot, the first time the prize is awarded posthumously.

2005

OCTOBER

Les Échelles du Levant (The Ports of the Levantine) (Gringoire, 1939) is published by Denoël under the title *Le Maître des âmes (Master of Souls)*.

2006

DECEMBER 16

Suite Française (Chatto & Windus, translated by Sandra Smith) is named Book of the Year by the *Times* of London.

2007

MARCH

Chaleur du sang (Fire in the Blood) is published by Denoël.

DECEMBER 19

Suite Française (Chatto & Windus, translated by Sandra Smith) is named Book of the Year by the British Independent Booksellers Association.

2008

Suite Française has been translated into thirty-eight languages and sold more than 1,300,000 copies worldwide. Nearly all of Irène Némirovsky's work has been rediscovered and continues to be translated into many languages.

Translated from the French by Garrett White

Fiction by Irène Némirovsky translated by Sandra Smith

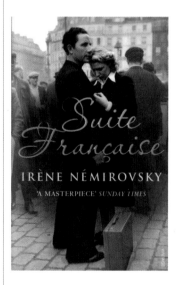

Cover of the British edition of *Suite Française.*

TOP
Michel Epstein and Paul Epstein,
at Chez Martin, Avenue George V,
Paris, n.d.

BOTTOM
Irène Némirovsky with
Michel (at left) and Paul Epstein, n.d.

ABOVE AND OPPOSITE
Irène Némirovsky and her daughter,
Denise Epstein, n.d.

ABOVE
Denise Epstein and her uncle,
Paul Epstein, ca. 1933

OPPOSITE
Denise Epstein, ca. 1933

Irène Némirovsky, ca. mid-1930s

Denise Epstein, ca. mid-1930s

ABOVE
Denise and Élisabeth Epstein, n.d.

OPPOSITE
Irène Némirovsky
and Denise Epstein, n.d.

ABOVE
Denise and Élisabeth Epstein
with Renée Michaud (left),
daughter of Cécile Michaud, n.d.

OPPOSITE
Élisabeth Epstein, 1942

the Virgins

BY IRÈNE NÉMIROVSKY

— INTRODUCTION —

"The Virgins" is the last work by Irène Némirovsky published during her life-time. When it appeared in the literary and political weekly publication *Présent* on Wednesday, July 15, 1942, the novelist had been arrested the Monday before and had spent two nights at the police headquarters in Toulon-sur-Arroux, fifteen kilometres from Issy-l'Évêque. She was about to be deported to the internement camp at Pithiviers, in the Loiret region. Feeling "calm and strong," she was preparing herself for incarceration and sent her family these few loving words: "I shower my darling daughters with kisses." This separation was the brutal consequence of decrees by the Secretary General of the Vichy Police, René Bousquet, ordering the French authorities to round up "stateless Jews" and hold them in camps in the Occupied Zone, in order to organize their "transfer" to "the Eastern territories," in other words, to deport them. Irène Némirovsky would only remain at Pithiviers for twenty-four hours, just long enough to become registered among the one hundred and nineteen women who, at dawn on July 17, would be sent to the Nazi concentration camp at Auschwitz-Birkenau in Poland. Had she been granted French citizenship, it might have perhaps delayed her departure; it would not have prevented it.

"The Virgins," like "A Happy Marriage," was intended for publication in the weekly journal *Gringoire*, where seven short stories and one novel by Némirovsky had been published under a pseudonym—necessary after the *Statut des Juifs* (laws regarding the Jews) came into effect in October 1940. It is not known why Horace de Carbuccia, the director of the newspaper, stopped offering his help after 1941. *Gringoire*, which had become an anti-Semitic rag, could undoubtedly no longer afford the paradox of an act of generosity. Because of this, André Sabatier, Némirovsky's editor and friend, sent her last two short stories to *Présent*, a weekly newspaper created by Jean Mistler in December 1941. "A Happy Marriage" would not be published until February 23, 1943, more than six months after Némirovsky's death.

Despite being a supporter of Maréchal Pétain (after the defeat of 1940, Mistler submitted the bill to the National Assembly that gave total power to Pétain), *Présent* was infinitely more moral than *Gringoire*. It did not contain any of the anti-Jewish diatribes, opinions of informers, or odes to collaboration that had become habitual in de Carbuccia's paper. It even had one of the best official literary supplements during the Occupation. Kléber Haedens, who had come from *Action française*, also published in it, along with certain future names from the Communist Resistance, such as Roger Vailland and Claude Roy.

The tragic circumstances that surround the publication of "The Virgins," under the extremely moving pseudonym of Denise Mérande, an allusion to the author's daughter and to her editor, Robert Esménard, leads us to a different interpretation of this story about a mother and her daughter who go to live in a village in the "real French countryside." "Look at me," moaned Camille. "I am alone like you now, but I have not sought or chosen solitude; mine is the worst kind of solitude, formed of bitterness and humiliation, the result of having been abandoned, betrayed." Such resigned anger recalls the despondency of the former Russians condemned by Bolshevism, as Némirovsky described them, in 1931, in *Les Mouches d'automne (Snow in Autumn)*: "Look, we're all alone, abandoned like dogs…"

And so twenty-five years had passed between the Russian Revolution and the National Revolution, and still the stateless Némirovsky had not been granted French citizenship. She remained eternally in exile, seeking the "refuge" that literature alone was able to provide. It was to be a precarious and illusory refuge, but one that endures, in spite of the "taste of burnt ashes" of happiness in ruins.

—OLIVIER PHILIPPONNAT

They had loved each other: but they hadn't been happy living together. They were both passionate and jealous, each as incapable of making concessions and being content as the other. Once married, they had lovers' quarrels; their existence was full of tempestuous conflicts that always ended in tender and passionate reconciliations. They had met when they were twenty; now they were forty-five. She had been extremely beautiful, but, unfortunately for her, she had one of those troubled faces whose lines and bitter expression even make-up couldn't manage to hide. After she had her daughter late in life, a child she cherished but had not really wanted, even her body, once so magnificent, had grown heavy and shapeless. Her husband still looked young. Endowed with a restless, adventurous nature, he hadn't been able to settle down in France. He had traveled all over the world. Whenever possible, his wife went with him. They were not well off. There were hard times. He ended up finding work in Morroco for a few years; he was an architect. Age was creeping up on him, and with it, luck and wisdom, he used to say, laughing. He was almost wealthy; the bad times faded from their memories. Then, he left her for his mistress.

The woman and child were returning home now, just the two of them.

The woman hoped to find refuge with one of her sisters, a primary school teacher in a small village in the center of France. It was snowing, and there had been some sort of misunderstanding about the time of the train, so no one was waiting at the station for the two travelers: my mother and me.

I was seven years old. I didn't understand anything that was happening. I clung to my mother's full skirt. I was shivering. I watched the translucent snowflakes fall; a workman's colored lantern made them change from a soft, shimmering green to a deep blood-red. While my mother took care of the luggage, I was left alone in a narrow, bare waiting room where a stove gave off a strong heat. Then I left the station, I remember, and crossed a small, very dark square surrounded by silent houses. A car took us a few kilometers further through a desolate countryside. The snow-covered fields sent a muted glow up towards the dark sky. I could make out some farms along a frozen lake, a crumbling wall, fir trees that looked enormous to me; the wind whistled through their branches causing a continuous, musical, plaintive vibration, like the kind you hear coming from telegraph wires on cold, winter days. I was crying very quietly. My mother saw my tears, forced herself to smile at me. She stretched out her hand and tenderly stroked my hair; her hand was burning hot and I could feel her quick, irregular pulse against my forehead. I was surprised and said, "You're so hot, Mama. And I'm freezing."

She said nothing.

The journey lasted nearly half an hour; the roads were bad. Time seemed to go by very slowly and my sadness deepened with every passing moment. Finally, the car stopped and Mama looked up.

"We're here, Nicole," she said.

A door opened, and from inside came light, warmth, the glow of a red fire, the sound of friendly voices and laughter, and a sweet smell I can still remember: it was a thick country soup, a sort of stew that had most likely been cooking all day over a wooden fire, in the old-fashioned way; the crackling of that wood fire, its smell, the slightly sweet aroma of celeriac strongest of all, seeped into my frozen little body, filling it with the most extraordinary sense of comfort. I was still standing in the dark, in the cold, I hadn't even crossed the threshold of that beautiful kitchen, and already the past, my father, the sun in Morocco, the journey, and my tiredness had faded. I had almost shed my grief. Above my head, women were crying and kissing each other. I watched them shyly; there were three of them who gathered around my mother. They looked old to me; one of them was short and chubby with big fat cheeks that trembled a bit; the other was tall and thin, with grey hair pulled tightly back; the third one—my Aunt Alberte—wore large round glasses balanced on her little turned-up nose. My mother loved this sister a lot. Whenever she talked about Alberte, it was as if she were still a young girl, yet she hadn't seen her for twenty years. I was astonished to hear her call her "Alberte, my little Alberte, my darling little sister." She seemed such an old spinster. I found out later that one of the other two women was a distant relation and the other a childhood friend of my mother's. The fat woman was called Blanche and the thin one Marcelle; I've forgotten their last names. Blanche worked in the village post office, Marcelle was a primary school teacher like my aunt. She had come to spend the Christmas holidays with Blanche. It was December 23. They had set up a pine tree in the living room for me, decorated with tinsel, toys, and candy. They took me in to show me how nice it was, but I couldn't see anything: I was asleep on my feet. In the kitchen, the table had been set; everything was bright, warm, and shining. I had a few spoonfuls of burning hot soup, then fell into a deep sleep. When I woke up, I was laying on a little sofa bed, in my aunt's bedroom. The door to the dining room had been left open and I could see the four women sitting near the fire; it must have been very late. At first they had spoken in low voices, so they wouldn't wake me up, then they forgot I was there and I could hear every word. My mother was telling them how my father had gone off with his mistress. Her words were interspersed with tears, sighs, curses.

"Hush, Camille, hush, you're just causing yourself pain," my aunt said, with pity.

"No, let me be, you're wrong, it makes me feel better," replied my mother. "All of this has been choking me…"

I saw her place her hand on her throat as if she were, in reality, feeling the physical sensation of suffocating. Her tears were flowing.

"He made me too unhappy," she said. "You don't understand, you can't understand…I loved him too much. I think it's a sin to love a man that much, even your own husband. At least, *I* felt guilty. It was too much. I was obsessed with him. If you only knew what he put me through! I followed him to godforsaken places where no other European woman would have ever agreed to live. That was when he was building a palace for some minor African dictator. But that place wasn't even the worst. There were only a few native women to make me jealous. But in Casa…You don't know what it means to 'live in fear.' To wake up thinking, 'He's not here any more. He's gone and will never come back.' To wait for him. And wait for him some more. The violent, almost desperate joy at seeing him: 'He's home, at last. At least he's still here today.' You see, he wasn't unfaithful like most husbands who chase after women; he was like a dog who always ends up finding its way back home again. But I knew—I knew that one day he would leave for good. He never tried to hide it. 'You've held on to me for twenty-five years, my darling,' he would say. 'That's an amazing feat. But, one of these days, I'm going to run off.' He wasn't actually mean, no, but he was so difficult, rebellious; he had the true nature of an adventurer. He would sometimes look at me in a kind of a daze, as if he really didn't know who I was, as if he were thinking: 'What the hell is *she* doing here?' Our child? Well, men like him don't have any fatherly feelings in their hearts. I can't criticize him, though. *I'm* the guilty one. I never should have married him, never. We were both twenty, but he already understood himself. He knew the kind of family he'd come from. His father had gone off the same way, one fine day, leaving his family behind; he just disappeared; no one ever knew what became of him. 'I don't care about money; I don't like cards, or wine, or women,' my husband used to say. 'But I have one passion: change. To leave behind a former life, like a snake sheds its skin. I'm warning you now that I'm going to hurt you.' But I, well, I didn't want to believe it. My God, my God, why didn't I do the same as you, Alberte? Why didn't I remain alone and at peace, with no man in my life, like you? I look at you and I envy you. Alberte, do you realize exactly how lucky you are? Love is so awful, it's such a lie!" exclaimed my poor mother.

"But," the chubby Blanche said softly, "not all marriages are…"

"It's life that's so dreadful. You keep yourselves to yourselves and you're right. Life only brings pain, distress, corruption, hurt. It's men who say that a woman has no life if she has no love. But you live alone and are happy, aren't you? Look at me. I am alone like you now, but I have not sought or chosen solitude; mine is the worst kind of solitude, formed of bitterness and humiliation, the result of having been abandoned, betrayed. I have no profession, nothing to keep my mind busy and fill my heart. My child? She makes me so sad; she's a living memory that haunts me. But you're all happy."

There was a rather long silence. My Aunt Alberte stood up to see to the fire. She spent a long time blowing on the wood that refused to light.

"They've sent me damp firewood," she complained. "Can you hear it crying?"

There was, in fact, a whistle, a hiss, a plaintive meowing coming from the fireplace. I listened, fascinated, and imagined that the wood really was crying, that the pieces of birch, cherrywood, and oak were shedding tears in large, silvery drops.

"My poor Camille," my aunt finally said, "I must admit that I've never envied your life. I am perfectly happy, it's true. I have a profession that interests me, just enough money to be comfortable. I like children; I like teaching. I enjoy living in the countryside. What is really good here, you'll see, is that this is the real countryside, a bit isolated perhaps, but not a little provincial backwater where people can't wait to hear the latest gossip. Nature is very beautiful. And, as you can see, I have my house."

The others agreed with her.

"Yes, Camille, it's true that you do not set a very good example for love," said Marcelle. "Let's not go as far as to say 'marriage,' but love. As for me, I wouldn't have been able to bear that kind of life. Everything you had to put up with… At the beginning, you were happy, of course."

"I've never been happy," my mother quickly protested. "We'd only been married for five months when I found out he was cheating on me. Then again, at the start of my pregnancy. You can't know, but a woman feels so weak then, so anxious. She needs someone there to reassure her. You couldn't understand. But I…well, I knew he was cheating on me and that there was nothing to be done: I could leave him or close my eyes to it, it was my choice. I loved him, so I accepted everything. Oh, no, no! I can't even say that I was ever happy."

The spinsters murmured affectionate words to console her.

"Come over here, come and lie down by the fire, my poor Camille," my aunt said softly. "Don't worry, we'll take care of you, we'll make you forget those awful times. Isn't it nice that we're all together again, just like we used to be? How strange life is! Do you ever think that for each of us, there is one specific moment when something happens that bends our destiny in a certain direction? You've often told me about your first encounter with your terrible husband, Camille."

"Yes," said my mother. "He was passing through our little town. He was going to see the church, and my mother had sent me to buy some pink thread at the shop. As I was leaving the house, I looked at myself in the mirror. I didn't like the way my hat looked, so I went back and put on my new one, and as I went out, Henri and I met right at our doorstep. We looked at each other, we fell in love... If it had been five minutes later, he would have been on one side of the street and I on the other; our paths would never have crossed, and I would have had a peaceful life, like you, until I grew old."

"It was the same for me," said the chubby Blanche, laughing. "I can also remember the exact moment that changed my life. I've never told you about it; it was too embarrassing. I was twenty years old, I was in love with... Ha! I won't tell you who it was. It's too late now. He's dead now. He left five children and his widow without a penny. A tall, flat-chested redhead. I sometimes see her when I go to visit my parents. Well, one day, I knew he was going to... propose to me... ask me to... Finally"—she let out a little giggle—"you know, a woman is never wrong about these things. I knew he was going to ask me to marry him. We were alone, we were both shy. He came up to me and at that very moment, I felt the shoulder strap of my camisole break. I was wearing a light blouse with lace panels that was in fashion at the time, and if my camisole fell, he'd be able to see my breasts. Now of course, we weren't like the brazen young girls of today. The very idea of letting a man see your breasts was awful! But, and I'm telling you this in confidence, I do think that if I'd had perfect breasts... Alas! I've always been rather chubby. So, I let out a cry and went all red. 'Don't come near me, Eugène,' I said, nearly in tears. 'Don't come near me!' He was so upset, the poor boy. 'But why, Blanchette? What's wrong? Are you afraid of me?' All I could do was say over and over again, arms crossed tightly over my chest, 'Go away. I'm telling you to go away!' He thought he was repulsive to me. He went away. The next day, he said hello to me very coldly, and never again, never again..."

She sighed.

"You see, if my blouse had been made of thicker material, I would have been a widow with five children and no money, like that poor redhead."

"If Cleopatra's nose had been shorter…," my aunt automatically replied.

Marcelle spoke up.

"I don't agree with you. It's not a matter of chance, but of instinct. When you ask one of my fellow teachers, a spinster like me, why she never got married, she replies, 'It just happened that way.' But no, that's not true. You're either suited to marriage or you're not. Suited to marriage, to love, to life even. You either want to live every minute passionately, or you want peace. For my part, I've always wanted peace. There was a time when I imagined I'd like to become a nun, but then I realized that it wasn't God I needed, but rather to be peaceful and alone, with my calm way of life, the routine I liked so much. A man! Good God! What on earth would I do with a man!"

"A man!" my mother repeated.

Then, after a silence, she added, "You're right, Marcelle. It's not a matter of chance, but of instinct, and even of desire. In the end, you always get what you have most passionately desired in this life, and that is our greatest punishment," she concluded.

I somehow sensed that Mama's tone, her way of speaking, everything had changed in the space of an hour. And, in fact, after that night, she was never the same; she became a country lady, a bit overweight, keeping busy in the kitchen, in the garden, growing vegetables, looking after the sick and tending the hens while my aunt was at her school. She was so content that a few years later, when my father wanted to come back and live with us, she replied, "My poor dear…That would be like asking a madman who's been cured to put his straightjacket back on."

My father died a few months later, suddenly, in some godforsaken hole, all alone.

The night I'm talking about has remained etched in my memory. I listened to those women talk. I watched the fire. I only half understood. I wanted to sleep, but their talking kept me awake. The thin Marcelle was knitting; I could hear the faint clicking of her steel needles and the words she said.

"As for me, I was the eldest of ten children, as you know. Ten children in a poor family, in a cramped house, well, you can imagine there wasn't much left to the imagination. I never dreamed of love, or marriage, or motherhood, not me. I knew the other side of that picture: my smug father who would go off to the café and leave my mother at home to "manage the kids." Manage them, yes, or work until she dropped, like she did, poor woman, dying giving birth to her eleventh child, the youngest, my brother Louis. So don't come talking to me about babies and how happy it makes you to take care of them, to pamper them. *I* know what it's really like, I've been there, I was the eldest, you know. *I* was the one who helped with the washing, the housework, making up the bottles. It was *me* they woke up when they cried, me who saw my poor exhausted mother, looking like a shriveled old woman when she was only thirty, without a single moment's rest, working in the house, working in the garden, all with some kid hanging on to her skirts, and another in her arms. Oh, no! I've never wanted a husband or babies. Thank God, I'm very content, I earn my living, I have my garden, my little house, the flowers, the animals. I was made for this kind of life and none other. And you were too, Blanche. If you had really been in love, you wouldn't have driven that young man away; you would have forgotten your modesty and even your fear of not seeming beautiful enough to him. If you had really been in love, you would have known instinctively that your love made you more attractive."

I was only a child, I was seven years old, but I was struck by how these spinsters said the words "love, marriage, motherhood, child." Their voices were so tender yet bitter!

"But you, Alberte," said my mother, placing her hand on her cheek while looking thoughtfully into the fire, "you seemed made for love. First of all, you were pretty…"

"Oh, no," protested my aunt.

"But you were. You were the prettiest of us all. Even now, your features are delicate and beautiful. If only you didn't wear those awful glasses…"

"My poor eyes," sighed my aunt.

"Ah! my dear Alberte, when you were seventeen, you loved to laugh, and have fun, and look attractive! Then, suddenly, you changed. Why?"

"Changed?" said my aunt. "What do you mean?"

"Well, you refused any invitations to parties and outings. You ran away from all the young men. Why? For a while, I thought you wanted to become a nun. Then I thought you'd fallen in love with someone who didn't love you back."

"I was never in love with anyone," said my Aunt Alberte, "and do you know why? I saw you, Camille, and I understood how unhappy you were. Of course, you thought you were hiding your life from your family, and, undoubtedly, Papa and Mama had no idea. But I did. You know that I always loved you so much. You were my favorite sister. Because of your romantic marriage, your determination to marry Henri against our parents' will, you became extraordinarily admirable to me. You were a living lesson and an example. If you had been happy, I would have done as you did. But, one day, I overheard you having an argument. Oh! It was horrible!"

"An argument…" said my mother quietly, and she shrugged her shoulders as if to say that there had been so many, and that they had meant nothing.

My aunt sat up straighter in her chair. She pulled off her glasses and I could see that she was, indeed, still pretty. Her delicate, proud, turned-up nose, her beautiful curved eyelashes and the firm, round shape of her cheeks clashed with her old-fashioned dress, the way her hair was done, like an old lady's, and the stiffness she had acquired, no doubt from the way she held herself when teaching: very straight, towering over the school children, the focal point of their attention.

"Oh! But I'm sure you can't have forgotten *that* argument, Camille. In any case, it made an extraordinary impression on me. It was…"

She broke off.

"But you're not drinking your mulled wine," she exclaimed, reproachfully.

She picked up a glass filled with a liquid that gave off the rich, warm aroma of cinnamon and spirits. My mother sipped at it. My aunt continued.

"You had been married for a year, I think; I was visiting you, in Paris. You had never quarreled in front of me, and I had never imagined that married people could have a relationship that was different from the one our parents had: something unutterably wonderful and peaceful that seemed to me the very essence of love. I was seventeen then, and I would say to people, 'As for me, *I* will never make a marriage of convenience, I will marry for love, like my sister Camille.' And then one night…"

She still shuddered at the memory. She hunched her shoulders and stretched out her hands towards the fire, trembling.

"You went out to a concert one evening, but I stayed at home because I had a cold. The sound of angry voices woke me up. My bedroom was right next to yours. I could hear you, Camille, saying such terrible things…Oh! They still send shivers down my spine when I think of it. You kept saying over and over again in a monotonous, moaning voice, like a lament: 'I want to die, Henri, I want to die.' I never found out exactly what had happened between you, but it was something to do with another woman, and he…he didn't try to defend himself or console you. He laughed, the monster! Such a cruel laugh, so arrogant, so pitiless that if I hadn't been a girl, I would have smashed his face in. That horrible man! Heartless! Then you both started shouting, hurling abuse at each other, and I listened, my heart pounding, overwhelmed by fear and pity. My poor Camille…My dear sister…That night, he hit you. I could hear your cries. I covered my ears. I buried my head in the pillows, I hid under the covers to try to block out the moans, the cries, but they haunt me even today. My God, I thought, is this how love ends? Kisses, caresses at first, and then beatings? And a woman can reach a point where she loses all self-respect! Forgive me, Camille, I know that you still loved him and that you would have rather died, as you often said, than admit the truth to the family, but all the same, all the same, such self-abasement, from you, you who were so proud! I dreaded the next day. I was prepared to tell you, 'Leave him. Come with me, come back home. I'll be good to you, I'll work to support you…' Well, in fact, the same thing I'm telling you today," my aunt concluded, speaking very softly. "Poor Camille! You suffered so much, but that night, you did me a great favor. The following day, I went home. I didn't dare say anything to you, and, besides, you didn't encourage people to confide in you. 'I'm happy, my dear little sister,' that's what you told me then. Time passed, but the terrifying impression of that night remained so vivid to me that whenever a man spoke of love, I heard your moaning, your cries, his laughter, and men filled me with horror. That's why I never got married. And as for a marriage arranged by our parents, I refused. But you, you've forgotten that night…"

They all fell silent for such a long time that I nearly fell asleep. My eyes started to close; then I was awakened by a sigh. I automatically looked over at my mother. She had finished the mulled wine, and bit of color had risen to her cheeks. She seemed relaxed, mysteriously calm and detached from everything. She sighed again, two or three times.

"I haven't forgotten, Alberte. That night, if you only knew…But you couldn't understand. You have to be a woman, you have to have become a woman, you see," she said quietly, her voice sounding secretive and almost ashamed. "You have to have had a young lover, to understand. Well, yes, he did swear at me, he did hit me. He humiliated me. But afterwards, oh, Alberte, innocent, naive Alberte, if you had come into our room, you would have seen how our kisses were even sweeter, different to the bland kisses you were describing a moment ago, that Papa and Mama gave each other. Alberte, I told you that I have never been happy, and that's true, absolutely true, but…What I'm describing isn't happiness. It's the taste of passion that love alone can give to life, the taste of ripe, succulent fruit, tinged with bitterness, the taste of young lips…"

"The taste of burnt ashes in the end," Marcelle said harshly.

"Yes, but…you don't understand. Love is born of pain, is fueled by tears. That night, Alberte, was perhaps the most beautiful night of my life. I don't mean it was the happiest, but it was the most beautiful, the night I felt the most fulfilled. I cried, and he drank in my tears. And I can still hear his gentle breathing, the soft panting sound that escaped from his lips. You say, 'You accepted everything because you still loved him.' But when you say those words, 'You loved him,' they sound dreary and cold. But to me…Oh! I don't know whether I loved him or not. It wasn't even really a question of love. I needed the sound of his voice, of his footsteps, needed the way he touched the back of my neck, the feel of his hand when he struck me, the taste of his kisses. It was a need as powerful as the need for salt, or food, or water."

It was strange. The words my mother spoke were weak and clumsy, but her voice was steady, devoid of passion. You would have truly said that there remained not a trace of passion in her. But she had the inimitable prestige of experience. She spoke to these elderly women as if she were a brilliant musician, an artist, a creative genius and they were little young ladies at boarding school playing *Clair de Lune* on the piano, stumbling, hitting the wrong keys and sighing with regret. At times, when she spoke my father's name, her mouth moved in a strange way, something between a bite and a kiss.

I think that for the first time in her life, she was *speaking* her love. She loathed any woman whom she deemed a potential rival; she had no female friends. But these three elderly country ladies were no threat: they would not steal her precious man. She trusted them; she began by speaking reluctantly, then she let herself be carried away by the wave of memories. And the more she spoke, the more she let go of love; it poured from her heart like perfume escapes from an open flask. I am certain that from her first night in France, she began to forget my father.

She continued, her voice full of pity.

"Of course, you couldn't understand," she said. "That's why you didn't get married, Marcelle, because you were horrified by your mother's life: a large family… no money…Of course, that's frightening. I knew your mother. I remember that unhappy woman, always pregnant, exhausted by the children. But if you only knew…Listen, when my little girl was born, I was breastfeeding her; my breasts were sore and cracked. It's a kind of pain you can't even imagine; you'd think someone was stabbing you with a sharp knife and cutting your the breast in half as if it were a piece of fruit. And yet, when the milk flowed, sometimes mixed with blood, and went into the mouth of the little baby that I had created…Ah, my poor Marcelle!…What can I say? That's what life is, real life."

My mother fell silent. I could hear the clink of the empty glass as she put it back down on the table. Her hair had come undone; it was thick hair, long, rather straight, black, with strands of gray. She had a beautiful face that I can still picture: wrinkles, a sad expression, hollow cheeks, as furrowed as a field in autumn. The women around her said nothing.

Blanche, the sweetest one, sighed.

"Of course…"

She broke off.

"I'll leave that pleasure to others my dear," Marcelle said proudly, gritting her teeth, "of that I can assure you."

"But you just said," exclaimed Aunt Alberte, "you said…"

"That I had been unhappy," my mother broke in. "That's true. How I envy you. I envy your peaceful existence, but…my life was complete, can you understand, I was fulfilled, but you…you never had anything."

Then Alberte, my Aunt Alberte, dropped her knitting, covered her eyes and, suddenly, burst out sobbing.

My mother, astonished, upset, stood up awkwardly and went over to her.
My aunt pushed her away.

"What is it, my darling Alberte? I know, I understand, you feel sorry for me, you're crying…"

"Sorry for *you*?" replied Alberte. "Oh, no! Not for you, Camille."

Her voice was filled with painful resentment.

"My poor sister, you never should have told us all this."

Translated from the French by Sandra Smith

NOTES *for*

CAPTIVITY

BY IRÈNE NÉMIROVSKY

INTRODUCTION

Notes relating to the composition of *Captivity*, the intended third section of *Suite Française*, were written by Irène Némirovsky between March 6 and March 31, 1942. They comprised a total of thirty-eight pages, of which only twelve have survived, and were among the manuscripts and rough drafts brought back to Paris by André Sabatier on April 3, or, at a later date, by Julie Dumot, the governess named the legal guardian of Denise and Élisabeth Epstein "if worst came to worst."

Four months before Némirovsky was arrested on July 13, 1942, *Tempête en juin (Storm in June)*, the first section of her master-piece, had been well and truly completed. But the second section, *Dolce*, was still far from having found the shape that her readers would see at the end of 2004. At the time, the romance between Lucile and Bruno, the high point of the novel, was still envisaged as the subject of a short story titled *"Nuit et Songes"* ("Night and Dreams"). It is a story of love doomed by the couple's instinctive feeling that they are too different from

each other. That it ultimately finds a place in the novel is due to the fact that from the end of fall 1941, even the weekly magazine *Gringoire*, which agreed to publish Némirovsky's works under a pseudonym, reneged on its commitment. In the winter of 1942 came the moment of painful realization: Irène Némirovsky would not be able to return to Paris, publish her novels, become French, and henceforth she would live in perpetual fear of being arrested. Ending up in a concentration camp, the fate in store for the undesirable immigrants in *Les Chiens et les Loups (Dogs and Wolves)*, the last novel published under her name in 1940, was, therefore, a premonition.

From this point on, Némirovsky understood the nature of the French only too well: the spirit of their language, which she assimilated to the highest level, had become the least valued criteria of national dignity. The "sincere and slightly mocking tenderness" which she used to describe the French in April 1940 gave way to "hatred" and "scorn." Hence the bitter reflections "on the state of France" that would contribute to the posthumous

success of *Suite Française:* "My God! What is this country doing to me?" Such thoughts continue: "For the French, freedom was like an old wife whose charms had faded. She has just died; they are inconsolable."

It is not possible to say what shape *Captivity* might have taken simply by reading these notes. The novelist was struggling to choose one plot from among the "vague ideas for various chapters" that filled her imagination. Would heroism transform Hubert into a member of the Youth for Maréchal Pétain? Would the conceited Corte devote himself to the National Revolution or become the "apostle of the resistance"? How is it possible to know "amid such chaos"? Everything depended on circumstances. It is remark-able that from Issy-l'Évêque, the village where she had taken refuge in 1940, Némirovsky was able so keenly to sense what several generations of historians would ultimately confirm: the inglorious ambiguity of French public opinion under the Oc-cupation. But equally remarkable is the way that she so precisely pinpointed the secret theme of *Suite Française:* the instinct of the individual to resist the ideologies of the collective, ideologies that were triumphant from Moscow to Vichy. "The greatness of the individual does not at all consist in being submissive, quite the contrary: despite being weak, it consists of pitting the individual's strength against fate. And when he is victorious, he becomes a God, in the pagan sense of the term; even if he is defeated, if he has fought bravely, his destiny is the destiny of a hero."

As with nearly all of Némirovsky's novels, *Suite Française* has a moral dimension. It is a satire on History in progress, because History is a blind colossus, and because one novel is enough to cause it to stumble before it has the chance to trample us under foot. Even a posthumous novel.

—OLIVIER PHILIPPONNAT

CAPTIVITY
NOTES PARTS TWO AND THREE

…

My idea was to create a tragedy on several levels; first, the idea that's going around (cf. *Varouna* Julien Green[1]) that our destinies all depend on each other. But this link must never be forced, because it would become mechanical. Secondly, *a panoramic vision of people and places… intensely vivid, inexhaustible stirring*[2] (it is possible that "Storm" may only be a prelude. It must be. That doesn't mean I can do it). Thirdly (and this is what seems so simple, yet is the most difficult) need to create a human story, smthng about which you can't say: *and then*[3] *Sacha fell in love with Boria,*[4] and so forth.

The only thing I see in it is friendship, a very beautiful, very powerful friendship, that extends to sacrifice, and is devoted to a great cause, but careful! Mustn't be taken in by it. Like everything, it must be true, that is to say, *not in the expected way,*[5] with sulking, misunderstandings, miscomprehensions [sic], etc. [T]his friendship naturally links Hubert and Jean-Marie. S[ee] if I should make Jean-Marie younger? I think he is twenty-six and Hubert is seventeen. I think maybe twenty-two or even

twenty-one compared to Hubert's seventeen would be better. That would be in '40, which in '42 or '43, alas, perhaps '44, '45 and '46 even, *Oh God,*[6] would make Jean-Marie twenty-four and Hubert twenty. Then love. First Jean-Marie and Brigitte. When Jean-Marie dies (and he must die willingly, and influenced by Philippe, Philippe's sacrifice which, for some mysterious reason, leads him to it) so, when Jean-Marie dies, Brigitte and Hubert end up falling in love.

…

Relationships between these characters. First, naturally, there must be some joint action which here could be simply an attempt to save the country, but each of them would do it as they think best: Hubert would be a "Jeune du Maréchal" [member of the Youth for Pétain Group], or smthng like that. Jean-Marie for the English. To think that twenty years from now all these trends will be so clear, and now, it's such chaos. Oh, well…

1 Green, Julien. *Varouna.* (Paris : Plon, 1940).
2 Original in English. —Trans.
3 Original in English. —Trans.
4 Original in Russian. Boria is a diminutive of Boris. —Trans.
5 Original in Russian. —Trans.
6 Original in English. —Trans.

1.

Hubert, because of Arlette, is thrown in jail, where he meets Benoît and Jean-Marie.

2.

Benoît is shot: he attacked a German; he hates them all because Madeleine fell in love with one, after having fallen in love with Jean-Marie.

3.

Jean-Marie is in jail because he was arrested for hiding weapons, etc. (cf. story of the son of M's friend).

   Hubert and Jean-Marie meet. The heroic death of Benoît finally makes a man of Hubert.

4.

Corte, writing solely out of vanity, hysteria, etc., pushes people into the most dangerous escapades without realizing it. It would even be rather amusing if he were on the right side, but wouldn't it surely be better if it were the wrong one? I'll have to see. He could first be wildly enthusiastic, passionate, about the National Revolution, and, then, annoyed because no one gave him any credit, he'd become the apostle of the resistance, while keeping himself safely on the sidelines, from abroad, for example.

5.

His attitude towards Jules Blanc.

6.

The family of Jules Blanc. His misery. Brigitte who definitely is not his daughter but the daughter of his mistress (I can't see the type, can't picture the social background). Brigitte winds up at the hospital, then at the Michauds'.

That leaves the workers, the Penitent Children, the Bank directors, and Charles Langelet to sort out (or rather, Langelet's fortune). I think I'll have to get rid of Langelet, unfortunately (that could make a long short story…) and in his place, I'll put Jules Blanc.

This second part must finish with the three heroes banding together, for the common good.

…

Let's assume that Corte, from Portugal or Canada, carries out a frenzied campaign to set up an "organization to liberate France," or smthng of the sort. Jean-Marie has already devoted his heart and soul to it. It wouldn't be bad to contrast these people who live cautiously abroad earning honor and money by preaching resistance with those who stand up and take the beating.

…

But I would like (for this I'd have to consult the Bolchies. Leave it for the third book just in case, gives me some space) I would like the Penitent Children to kill off my Corte for me.

Meanwhile (second book) the directors are involved in big business deals.

…

Now, don't forget what is good in *War and Peace*, e.g., it's in the middle of all these incredible upheavals that people carry on with their lives more or less normally and, in the end, only think about surviving, loving, eating, etc. Besides, all this is a matter of emphasis. It is the "egotistical" personal life that must be stressed.

…

So the book should start with the arrival of the Germans (symbolic, it's not the first time…) in Benoît's village, and finish either by their leaving (but that would be too good to be true) or by smthng that shows the friendship between Jean-Marie / Hubert (first I had thought: love scene Jean-Marie & Brigitte, then feared it would be too banal). In reality, should have both, some dangerous outing like with Jean-Marie and Hubert, then Jean-Marie finds Brigitte again. That's when a child should be born. The second book should end with a birth.

…

Instead of the porcelain collector, I should have put Jules Blanc's visit to his mistress in the first book, which would have let me introduce Brigitte.

…

IN THE SECOND BOOK

1.

The Péricands—Jacqueline's First Communion. Hubert is jealous of Arlette, goes out to spy on her in spite of the rules, is thrown in jail.

2.

Arlette?

3.

The two bank directors do business with the Germans.

4.

Corte, after having exalted the National Revolution, gets frightened (or doesn't earn enough?), anyway, in a panic, flees abroad, and there writes an admirable book full of patriotism that stirs up all the young people, encouraging them to go and stand up and take the beating, and brings him a lot of glory and approval.

5.

Jules Blanc hides in a little village like Issy, doesn't understand what's happening to him and is killed like *what's his name*?[7]
A politician, I can't remember which one. Is it Jouhaux?[8] He could be killed by Blache and Ponpon. (Obviously, but now I'm digressing, it would be fantastic if Blache and Ponpon somehow get Langelet's money. But Lord, how? Unless there's a Revolution? Not likely. Or maybe, make Langelet Jewish. But even then...Alas, it looks impossible. That would be... *a dream*.[9])

6.

The Michauds represent intelligence, common sense, and honor and take in Brigitte. Jean-Marie does something great, tries at least. Also, that would only be good if his many qualities were described, and especially as if it had happened a hundred years ago. Yes, what's needed here is serenity. But when there's so little of it in your heart... *good*[10] for

7 Original in English. —Trans.
8 Léon Jouhaux (1879–1952), Secretary General of the CGT (French Trade Union), 1909–1947, arrested then deported to Buchenwald in November 1942. —Trans.
9 Original in English. —Trans.
10 Original in Russian. —Trans.

Tolstoy. He didn't give a damn. Yes, but as for me, I'm working on
burning hot lava. Right or wrong, I believe that this is what must
distinguish the art of our time from the rest, we are sculpting what
is happening at this very moment, we are working on burning issues.
It will all dissolve, of course, but that is exactly what is necessary
in contemporary art. If such an impression has any meaning, it is a
perpetual becoming, and not smthg already finished. Cf. cinema.

7.

The Penitent Children might be excellent murderers but afterwards they
must enjoy the most fantastic fate, *like snow falling on your head*.[11]
I could get rid of one of them through a violent death, and the other,
hailed as the savior of France, could become Arlette Corail's lover.
Mona, you are digressing, and for a long time now, some good critics
have seen in you a terrible inclination towards soap opera[12].

8.

The peasant farmers. Benoît kills a German. Madeleine runs away.
Cécile gets rich selling things on the black market.

9.

Charlie Langelet?

...

VAGUE IDEAS FOR VARIOUS CHAPTERS

1.

Arrival of the Germans (Easter, '41)

2.

First Communion for the Péricands (May '41)

---

11 Original in Russian, an idiomatic expression meaning "by surprise." —Trans.
12 Mona: One of Némirovsky's nicknames for herself. —Trans.

3.

Arlette (this life, alas, purely fictional) and Hubert's jealousy
(he's jealous of a German)

4.

The Michauds at war, or life in Paris in winter.
Then it isn't a First Communion but Christmas.

5.

Jean-Marie

6.

Jules Blanc Issy

7.

Jules Blanc's wife goes to look for Corte and Arlette.
Corte for the Natl. Revolution

8.

Arlette introduces the German to the director of the bank.
~~The German should sometimes be in Paris, sometimes in Issy?~~

9.

The Germans in the village (Arlette's German goes back to the village)

10.

~~Brigitte is alone~~ Brigitte

11.

Scandal around the Cortes, who clear out

12.

~~Brigitte at the hospital~~ Brigitte and her mother are taken
in by the Michauds

13.

~~The Michauds and life in Paris.~~
~~Right after Arlette, two chapters a)—the Michauds b)—Jean-Marie~~
Brigitte falls in love with Jean-Marie

14.

Madeleine and the German (at the Hôtel des Voyageurs)

15.

June 22.[13]

16.

Arlette and the directors share the money.

17.

Corte abroad

18.

~~The death of~~ Jules Blanc (the Hôtel des Voyageurs. When he is waiting for letters and all that)

19.

~~the Michauds take in Brigitte~~ The birthday party of three children.

20.

~~Arlette and Hubert in prison~~ Benoît

21.

Hubert in prison

22.

Jean-Marie in prison (relationship with the Germans)(?)

23.

Execution of Benoît

24.

Friendship of Jean-Marie and Hubert

25.

What about the workers? And the Penitent Children? If I do something with this, and I must, it's *in*.[14] The Penitent Children kill Jules-Blanc.

13 On June 22, 1941, Hitler launched his offensive in Russia. —Trans.
14 Original in English. —Trans.

26.

```
The death of the German, why not? Poor Sp.¹⁵ and Madeleine
```

27.

```
Madeleine runs away (Cécile and the black market). The workers!
What if she supplied food to Mme. Péricand?
```

28.

```
Love between Jean-Marie and Brigitte (beginnings)
```

29.

```
Dangerous expedition.
```

30.

```
Love between Jean-Marie and Brigitte (height of)
```

15 Sp: Probably Paul Spiegel, the German noncommissioned officer at Issy-l'Évêque who became Michel Epstein's friend. —Trans.

What if Langelet were called Laengelé, or smthg like that… How could it be done? I need his money, in some mysterious way, to be distributed among the workers and the Penitent Children, but that could be in the 3rd book. But, for that, there would at least have to be some kind of revolutionary movement. All in all, two things are needed for my book to hold together: 1) a Communist revolution in France that's very short-lived and 2) victory of the English. *Oh, God! Topsy*¹⁶ don't be blasphemous!¹⁷

…

In "Storm," what was good were the unexpected things: e.g.: the night of the cat, the forgotten father-in-law, Arlette and Hubert, Charlie stealing the gas… It was very original. Here, I can't picture anything like that: everything is predictable. But, after all, perhaps that's right. There's panic like in "Storm" that brings out what is mad, savage, in everything, what is contradictory in the human soul, provided the long imprisonment of *Captivity* has a different effect. First of all, cowardice. But let's be charitable. Next, the deepening of the soul. The fire spreads, burns stronger, devours the heart: the directors of the bank love money even more. Jean-Marie and Hubert become more passionately patriotic, or join a political party, perhaps… Madeleine is even more in love than she was with Jean-Marie: she becomes the German's mistress. Benoît has no qualms about killing.

16 Topsy: This is the nickname given to Irène Némirovsky by her English governess, Miss Matthews, which she used to sign her first published text, *Nonoche and the Clairvoyant* (*Fantasio*, August 1921). —Trans.
17 Original in English. —Trans.

1.

So for the Péricands: the father, the grandfather, <u>Philippe</u>,
<u>Hubert</u>, <u>the mother</u>, Jacqueline, Bernard, etc.

   <u>Philippe</u> influences the fates of Hubert, Jean-Marie, Brigitte.
<u>Hubert</u> [influences] Arlette, Brigitte, Jean-Marie, Benoît.

2.

<u>Arlette Corail</u> influences the two bank directors, and Hubert
[influences] Madeleine's German

3.

The two bank directors [influence] the German
(they have to fleece the German)

4.

<u>The Cortes</u> [influence] Benoît, Hubert; and Jean-Marie [influences]
Brigitte and Jules Blanc

5.

<u>Jules Blanc</u> [influences] Corte and the Penitent Children.

6.

The Michauds. <u>Jean-Marie</u> [influences] Philippe, Hubert, Brigitte,
Madeleine, Ben

7.

<u>The Penitent Children</u> [influence] Jules Blanc.

8.

<u>The peasant farmers</u> [influence] Benoît, Madeleine, Cécile
and the <u>workers</u>; Benoît [influences] the German, Hubert, Jean-Marie;
the workers [influence] Cécile and Mme. Péricand

9.

Charlie?

Must especially avoid proving anything. Here even less than anywhere else. Not that some are good and others are bad, not that one person is wrong and another is right. Even if it's true, especially if it's true. Depict, describe. Shakespeare. "It is probable that upon reading him for the first time, Goethe saw what he had always dreamed of and waited for in the world of art. To find, simultaneously, in the form best adapted to the human spirit, the most meaningful and expansive poetry combined with the truest and most detailed realism…to pass, in a few seconds, over the depths of the human soul on the solid bridge of words, to see passions collide like flashes of lightning on a stormy night, and finally to watch rise and spread all around this chaos of passion the calmest, purest, most serene sky ever recorded by human thought (Lord, what beautiful French)— here indeed was something to intoxicate the young Goethe.

"…Shakespeare…in the way his scenes are divided, offered an <u>immediate vision</u> that was extraordinarily true to life. It was no longer a question of using clever devices to bring people together in the same place… Everyone was there, jostling with each other along the streets of the city. <u>Everything both united and isolated them, frenetic events</u>

<u>threw them against one another,</u> and in the midst of their turmoil, their drifting, their loves, their betrayals, suddenly, as if they were listening to who knows what heavenly song coming from the woods and the branches, they stopped living in order to have their turn to sing, to whisper some lament or to give in to the lyrical delights of the most subtle and tender reverie."[18]

…

I'm worried a little about the way it's expanding. It must be kept, ~~if it's part of the thing~~ but get it organized.

On the other hand, which are the events that are typically "Captivity"?

Arrival and departure of the Germans in Issy.

The long lines on the streets of Paris (careful it's not '42 any more).

It's above all the atmosphere of Paris, winter, the snow still on the ground, green uniforms, the sad faces, worn-out clothes (*rough beards like tramps*[19]) and alongside this smthg like Martin's[20] the crowd, the laughter, a long line of people standing in the snow and wind who are not waiting to buy bread, or

wine, or meat, but a ticket to the movies.

Jules Blanc, it's at Issy that he dies, at the Hôtel des Voyageurs. In the same hotel lives Madeleine's German, who climbs out of the window at night to go and meet her.

In Issy-l'Évêque, the workers sell their calves, chickens, and pigs on the black market.

…

War and Peace is like an *Iliad*, the story of certain men, and an *Aeneid*, the story of a nation, compressed into one book.

Must make more of <u>*Peace*</u>, put peaceful little games in it. Now, must not forget that most of these descriptions are about people: love, the desire to earn money, jealousy, Hubert, but still, it would be appropriate to defend that.

…

<hr>

18 Excerpt copied from Edmond Jaloux, *Vie de Goethe* (Plon, 1933), pp. 66–67. Ellipses indicate where Némirovsky omitted words; "Lord, what beautiful French" is her insertion. —Trans.

19 Original in Russian. —Trans.

20 The bar on Avenue George V where Michel, Irène, and Alexandre "Choura" Lissianski were regulars. —Trans.

Naturally, the weakness, the only one in *War and Peace* in my opinion, is that T[olstoy] depicts authentic heroes. But it's the same if people ask me, what's it all about? Present a tableau, necessarily incomplete but the most extensive and the strongest one possible, about certain ordinary people (because everyone is ordinary) in extraordinary circumstances…

…

Yes, make sure that these extraordinary circumstances are always seen from the point of view of the hero. However, the arrival of the Germans stands apart, like a prelude. Is what I've done in Storm good, these Preludes and Finale that stand apart? Here, the first chapter will stand apart, and then what? June 22, again, and the end.

What I feel I most lack is one central theme. "Storm" was chaos; that holds up, but in "Captivity" smthg must take shape. It should be the attempts made to liberate France, on the one hand, even by different means, and on the other, the simplest and most banal experiences: the friendship between the two men, the love one of them feels for Brigitte. *Moments of happiness snatched.*[21] The hope of the young people who want to get on with their lives in spite of all the dangers.

…

Yes. Jean-Marie must either think or say: "The terrible upheavals like the one in June seem to leave nothing lasting in the soul of the individual; nothing except the great turmoil that has existed since the beginning of time. But undoubtedly this is just how the mind works: I would bet that during the mass exodus, any girl who got pregnant by her lover was mainly worried not about hunger or bombs, but about her lover, and whether or not he'd marry her."

Oh, a dinner party given by the Cortes, a dinner where they rail against the workers, the Jews, the lack of pleasures and the laziness that's taken hold of ordinary people, and by contrast: "But how did you manage to get hold of all of this [food]? It's amazing." "But darling, I manage somehow" (and Cécile, invisible and protective…).

For the French, freedom was like an old wife whose charms had faded. She has just died; they are inconsolable.

Jules Blanc, who, every day, in public meetings, organized Europe and the day of the debacle, forgets everything; he drops all of his important papers, secret files; he runs away with a suitcase containing two shoes that do not match, and his golf outfit.

Translated from the French by Sandra Smith

21 Original in English. —Trans.

Contributors

OLIVIER CORPET is Director and co-founder of the Institut Mémoires de l'Édition Contemporaine (IMEC). He is currently at work on a biography of Alain Robbe-Grillet, and is co-curating, with Robert O. Paxton, an exhibition on French literary life under the Nazi Occupation, scheduled to open at the New York Public Library in spring 2009.

EMMANUELLE LAMBERT is Head of Exhibitions and Fundraising at IMEC. She holds the *Agrégation* and a Ph.D. in Modern French Literature from the University of Paris VII.

PATRICK LIENHARDT is co-author, with Olivier Philipponnat, of *La Vie d'Irène Némirovsky*, the first comprehensive biography of the author of *Suite Française*, and *Roger Stéphane, enquête sur l'aventurier*, a biography of the founder of *L'Observateur* and a pioneer of cultural television in France. In 1998, he launched parutions.com, a daily webzine on literature and books.

DAVID G. MARWELL, Director of the Museum of Jewish Heritage – A Living Memorial to the Holocaust, received a Ph.D. in Modern European History from the State University of New York, Binghamton. Prior to his work at the U.S. Holocaust Memorial Museum in Washington, D.C., from 1997 to 2000, Marwell was Director of the Berlin Document Center and served as Chief of Investigative Research for the U.S. Department of Justice, Office of Special Investigations, where he was responsible for conducting historical and forensic research in support of Justice Department prosecution of Nazi war criminals. He has also served as an expert witness and consultant to the governments of Canada and Australia on war crimes prosecutions.

OLIVIER PHILIPPONNAT is co-author, with Patrick Lienhardt, of *La Vie d'Irène Némirovsky* and *Roger Stéphane, enquête sur l'aventurier*. *La Vie d'Irène Némirovsky* received the 2008 *Le Point* prize for biography, and will be published in the United States by Alfred A. Knopf in fall 2009. Philipponnat has also written prefaces to three novels by Irène Némirovsky, *Le Maître des âmes (The Master of Souls)*, *Chaleur du sang (Fire in the Blood)*, and *Les Mouches d'automne (Snow in Autumn)*.

SANDRA SMITH is a Fellow of Robinson College, University of Cambridge, England, where she teaches Literature and Translation. Born and raised in New York City, Smith has a Master's Degree from New York University, in conjunction with the Sorbonne. She is the primary English-language translator of the work of Irène Némirovsky. In 2007 her translation of *Suite Française* won the PEN/Book-of-the-Month Club Translation Prize and the French-American Foundation and the Florence Gould Foundation Translation Prize.

GARRETT WHITE is the founder of Five Ties Publishing and the former Director of Publications at the Whitney Museum of American Art and the Los Angeles County Museum of Art. He has edited and produced numerous books on literature, fine art, photography, architecture, and film, and is the translator of, among other works, *An Unspeakable Betrayal: Selected Writings of Luis Buñuel* and *Hollywood: Mecca of the Movies* by Blaise Cendrars.

IMEC is the most important nongovernmental foundation in France dedicated to preserving, publishing, and exhibiting the archives of modern and contemporary writers, artists, and publishing houses. Located in a state-of-the-art storage and research facility at the Abbaye de Ardenne, near Caen, Normandy, its more than 450 archives include those of Roland Barthes, Marguerite Duras, Michel Foucault, and the publishing houses Hachette, Flammarion, and Éditions du Seuil. (www.imec-archives.com)

THE MUSEUM OF JEWISH HERITAGE – A LIVING MEMORIAL TO THE HOLOCAUST in New York has welcomed more than a million visitors since opening in 1997. The museum's Core Exhibition focuses on Jewish life before, during, and after the Holocaust. Created as a memorial to those who perished in the Holocaust, the museum honors those who died by celebrating their lives—cherishing the traditions they embraced, examining their achievements and faith, and affirming the vibrant worldwide Jewish community that is their legacy today.

Acknowledgments

Neither the book nor the exhibition *Woman of Letters: Irène Némirovsky and Suite Française* would have been possible without the participation and support of Denise Epstein, and it is to her above all that I offer my most heartfelt thanks. Her watchful trust, enthusiasm, and encouragement have been deciding factors throughout the entire endeavor.

I am grateful as well to David G. Marwell, Director of the Museum of Jewish Heritage, Ivy Barsky, Deputy Director, and the MJH staff, whose dedicated commitment to the project never waivered.

I wish to thank the Cultural Service of the French Embassy in New York, in particular those in charge of supporting the book, first Fabrice Rozié, who provided the initial momentum, and later Fabrice Gabriel, who shepherded this Franco-American project to its completion.

Grateful acknowledgment is due to all those who participated in the development and production of this book, first and foremost to Irène Némirovsky's biographers, Olivier Philipponnat and Patrick Lienhardt, for providing us with their indispensable assistance in identifying and presenting the texts, documents, and photographs drawn from the Némirovsky archive, and for crafting a precise, authoritative, and lively chronology of Irène Némirovsky's life and work. Thanks also to Sandra Smith for her translations in this book, and for giving us the benefit of her intimate knowledge of the work of Irène Némirovsky following her award-winning English translation of *Suite Française* and many other writings by Irène Némirovsky.

I am indebted to my colleagues and collaborators at IMEC, in particular Nathalie Léger, Head of Publications, and Emmanuelle Lambert, Head of Exhibitions, and her team—especially Pierre Clouet and Caroline Dévé—who managed the entire project with dedication and professionalism.

I also wish to express my gratitude to Olivier Rubinstein, Director of Éditions Denoël and the fortunate publisher of the original French edition of *Suite Française*, who has followed this project with great interest.

Thanks as well to my old friend and colleague Garrett White, who was enthusiastic about the idea for this book from the beginning. I am pleased that it was this occasion that allowed us to undertake a joint effort between IMEC and Five Ties Publishing. Garrett was assisted in the production of *Woman of Letters* by Michael Femia, Amanda Thorpe, and designer Penelope Hardy, of PS New York, and her associate, Elizabeth Oh.

Finally, it is with great affection that I wish especially to remember Élisabeth Gille, Denise Epstein's sister, thanks to whom I first met Denise and came to know the work of Irène Némirovsky. It was the two of them together who gave me the great gift of choosing IMEC to conserve their mother's tremendous heritage.

—OLIVIER CORPET

PHOTO CREDITS

All photographs and documents from the Némirovsky
Archive are © 2008 Denise Epstein/IMEC
(www.imec-archives.com). Pages 7, 91, and back cover
© Harlingue-Viollet; pages 32, 35 (below), and 87
© Jean Roubier; page 48, photograph of Élisabeth Epstein
Gille, © Louis Monier; page 48, photo of Denise Epstein
taken by Pascale Butel © IMEC; portrait of "Zézelle,"
page 60, portrait of Irène Némirovsky, page 63, and
portrait of Irène Némirovsky with "Kissou," page 83,
courtesy of Tatiana Morozova; page 96 © Fortin & Cgnie.;
page 102 (lower left), reproduction of Irène Némirovsky's
last letter, courtesy of Archives du CDJC/Mémorial
de la Shoah/Collection Epstein, Paris, France; page 117
© G. L. Manuel Frères.

Five Ties Publishing, Inc., New York
www.fiveties.com

EDITORS
Olivier Corpet, Garrett White

ASSOCIATE EDITOR
Michael Femia

PROOFREADER
Amanda Thorpe

BOOK AND COVER DESIGN
PS New York
Penny Hardy, Elizabeth Oh
www.psnewyork.com

FIRST EDITION
© 2008 Five Ties Publishing, Inc.

Published on the occasion of the exhibition *Woman
of Letters: Irène Némirovsky and Suite Française* at the
Museum of Jewish Heritage – A Living Memorial to
the Holocaust, September 24, 2008 – March 22, 2009
www.mjhnyc.org

Woman of Letters: Irène Némirovsky and Suite Française
was made possible in part through the generous assistance
of the Cultural Service of the Embassy of France in the
United States.

"The Virgins" and "Notes for *'Captivity'*"
© Denise Epstein 2008

"Chronology of the Life of Irène Némirovsky"
© Olivier Philipponnat and Patrick Lienhardt 2008

Introductions to "The Virgins" and "Notes for *Captivity*"
© Olivier Philipponnat 2008

English translations of "Interview with Denise Epstein,"
"The Virgins," and "Notes for *Captivity*"
© Sandra Smith 2008

English translation of "Chronology of the Life of
Irène Némirovsky" © Garrett White 2008

Printed by Transcontinental Printing, Inc.,
Montreal, Quebec, Canada
www.transcontinental.com

Printed in Canada

ISBN 978-0-9794727-5-6